KU-160-119

A GREAT WEEKEND IN

AMSTERDAM

A GREAT WEEKEND IN AMSTERDAM

Wherever you are in Europe, you're never more than an hour or so away from Amsterdam by plane, so there's no excuse for not spending a few days in the city they call the 'Venice of the North', the 'city of tulips', the 'city of a hundred canals', the 'diamond capital' or the 'city of the golden century'. But, clichés aside, Amsterdam is like nowhere else on earth. Famed for its cheese, its tulips, its canals and its art museums, Amsterdam has something for everyone. The city's many faces are as varied as its districts which, though closely packed together, are all quite unique.

Amsterdam is a paradoxical place, conservative in some ways, pioneering in many others. This home of right-thinking Calvinists was the first city to establish a trade union for prostitutes, pass draconian laws against pollution from cars and legalise marriage between people of the same sex. Amsterdam's coffee-shops, where the sale and consumption of cannabis resin is permitted, and its highly mixed and apparently mutually accepting population of 145 different nationalities reflect the city's tolerant attitudes.

If there's one thing all Amsterdammers share, it's a love of trade, which sends them travelling all over the world to bring back the rare objects you find in the big antique shops on Spiegelstraat or the Rokin. But the city also has dozens of junk shops, which are fun to explore and also have some real bargains. Take advantage of your trip to buy all your garden bulbs or hunt down the last word in gadgets in the Jordaan district. You can buy cheap clothes here too, as long as you're not expecting the elegance of Paris or Milan.

With only 730,000 inhabitants – and 550,000 bicycles – Amsterdam is still a small city, enclosed by a network of canals linked to the North Sea. You can easily get around it on foot, amongst the elegant houses and numerous cafés, losing yourself in places that resemble a Van Goyen seascape or a genre painting by Jan Steen. It's then that you begin to understand why Amsterdammers use the word *gezellig* so often. This is an untranslatable word that's often used to convey the conviviality of their relaxed surroundings. It doesn't take long before Amsterdam's love of partying turns the streets into a colour carnival full of crazy outfits, pointed hats, purple-haired punks and young men swathed in leather. After you've watched one of these spontaneous shows, spent time admiring Rembrandt's painting of *The Night Watch* and Van Gogh's *Sunflowers* and are at last leaning on the counter of one of the city's 1,402 cafés or dancing under a club's hypnotic lights, you'll know you've touched the beating heart of Amsterdam.

Having glimpsed its true face, stammered out a few words in Dutch, tasted some of the thousand subtle flavours of *jenever*, watched one of the forty shows on offer every day of the week, rifled through all the market stalls and been to every museum in town, you'll know that there's only one thing left for you to do, and that's come back to Amsterdam.

How to get there

Spring and summer are probably the best seasons in which to get the most out of your weekend trip to Amsterdam, but you can never be absolutely certain of getting the better of the Dutch climate. In practice, it may be rainy and cold at any time of year.

July and August are not only the hottest months (21-26°C/70-79°F), they're also the period when most hotels charge low season prices. And if you can cope with bitterly cold, damp weather, Amsterdam is quite charming in the depths of winter, when the frozen canals bring to mind the works of the great 17th-century painters.

How to get there

Since cars are completely useless in Amsterdam, the quickest and most comfortable way to travel is by plane.

By plane

Amsterdam is a major European gateway and airlines periodically offer amazing deals that bring the price of a return ticket to significantly less than the price of a train or other overland journey. The permitted maximum allowance for luggage taken in the hold is 23kg/50lbs in economy class and 30kg/66lbs in business class. If you go over the limit you'll have to pay a surcharge calculated at a rate per kilo.

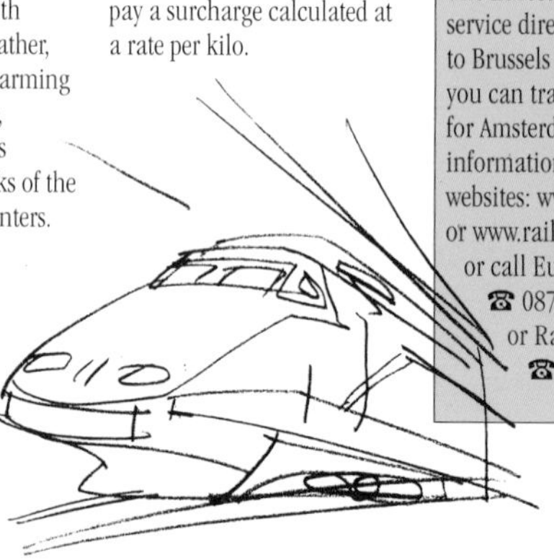

By train

If you'd prefer to travel by train, Amsterdam is only a few hours away from any major city in mainland Europe on the high-speed Thalys service, run by the French, Belgian, German and Dutch railways. You can book online on www.thalys.com or call them on ☎ 0033 836 35 35 36.

The Eurostar offers a fast service direct from London to Brussels or Paris where you can transfer to trains for Amsterdam. For more information log on to their websites: www.eurostar.com or www.raileurope.co.uk, or call Eurostar on ☎ 08705 186 186 or Rail Europe on ☎ 08705 848 84.

FLIGHTS FROM THE UK

Among the major carriers flying to Schiphol airport from the UK and Ireland are:

British Airways
www.british-airways.com
☎ 0845 773 3377
Frequent daily direct flights from the UK to Amsterdam.

British Midland
www.flybmi.com
☎ 0870 6070 555
Up to eight daily flights to Amsterdam from the UK.

Easyjet
www.easyjet.com
☎ 0870 6000 000
Regular daily flights from UK airports.

KLM
www.klm.com
☎ 08705 074 074
Regular flights to Amsterdam from 15 UK airports.

FLIGHTS FROM IRELAND

Aer Lingus
www.aerlingus.com
☎ 01 886 8888
Daily direct flights from Dublin and Cork.

FLIGHTS FROM THE USA AND CANADA

KLM/Northwest
www.klm.com / www.nwa.com
☎ 1 800 447 4747
Daily code-shared services from major airports.

Delta
www.delta-air.com
☎ 1 800 221 1212
Daily flights direct to Amsterdam from major airports.

TWA
www.twa.com
☎ 1 800 982 4141
Daily direct flights to Amsterdam.

Air Canada
www.aircanada.com
☎ 1 888 247 2262
Flies to Amsterdam via London.

INCLUSIVE BREAKS

Many tour operators offer 2 or 3 day weekend breaks at fixed prices which include transport and accommodation. Some of the best deals can be found in the travel sections of the weekend broadsheets, or your local travel agent should be able to assist you. The **Amsterdam Travel Service** (☎ 0870 727 5972 www.amsterdamtravel.co.uk) can plan and organise your entire itinerary for you. Other reputable agents include **Eurobreak** (☎ 020 8780 7700), **Bridge Travel** (☎ (0870) 727 5973) and **Destinations Europe** (☎ 01473 787160). You could also check current deals on the internet with **Expedia** (www.expedia.com), **Travelocity** (www.travelocity.com) or the **Travel Shop** (www.traveleshop.com)

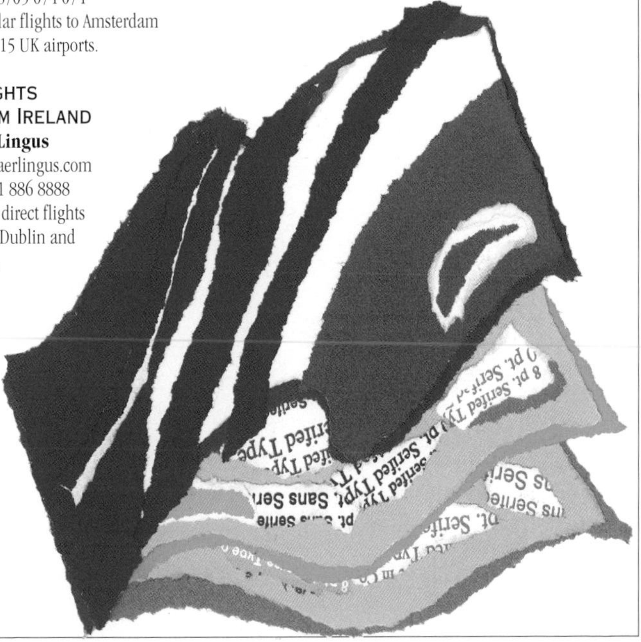

Flights from Australia and New Zealand

KLM flies direct to Amsterdam from Sydney, but it may be cheaper to find a flight with a stopover. From New Zealand, you can fly with Qantas via Sydney, and KLM offers a code share with Air New Zealand to Amsterdam via Los Angeles. All major airlines fly to Europe, and it's worth seeing a travel agent to work out the cheapest and most convenient route.

KLM
www.klm.com
☎ 02 9922 1555 (Australia)
☎ 09 309 1782
(New Zealand)

Qantas
www.qantas.com
☎ 13 12 11 or
02 9261 3636 (Australia)
☎ 09 357 8900 or
0800 808 967 (New Zealand)
Qantas flies daily from Sydney to Amsterdam, usually via London and an Asian airport. All flights from New Zealand go via Sydney.

British Airways
www.british-airways.com
☎ 02 9258 3300 (Australia)
☎ 09 356 8690
(New Zealand)
Daily flights from Sydney and other Australian cities, via London Heathrow.

From the airport to the city centre

Schiphol airport is 18km/ 11 miles southwest of Amsterdam. You have a choice of three modes of transport to take you to the city centre. Quickest and fastest is the train, which gets you to Amsterdam's central station in 20mins. Departures every 10mins until 12.30am and every hour between 1am and 6am, from the airport station located under the terminal. Ticket offices are open day and night (€2.95 one way, €5.22 return). A KLM bus to six of Amsterdam's grand hotels leaves the airport's main exit every half hour between 6.30am and 6pm. Buy your ticket from the driver, price €7.95. You can get a taxi from the airport direct to your hotel door for about €32. Journey time varies from 30mins to 1 hour.

Customs

As signatories to the Schengen agreement, the Dutch do not make systematic customs checks at their borders on nationals of the European Union. If you enter the country by car from Belgium,

you won't even notice. If you're travelling by train, however, your luggage may be searched by French or Belgian customs officials because of the drugs traffic. So beware: although possession of 5gm/1.5oz of marijuana is permitted in the Netherlands, it's entirely illegal once you cross the border.

In June 1999 duty-free allowances were abolished between EU countries, therefore there are no limits to the amount of goods you can bring back from a member state, as long as they are for your own personal use. If you enter the Netherlands from a non-EU country, however, you can only take with you 200 cigarettes or 50 cigars, 2 litres of wine, 1 litre of alcohol of more than 22°, 2 litres of less than 22°, 50cl of perfume, 25cl of eau de toilette and 500gm/1.1lbs of coffee. The import of firearms, amunition, knives, swords, etc. is illegal.

Getting used to the Euro

On 1 January 2002 the euro replaced the official currency of 12 European nations, including the Netherlands, and the guilder ceased to be legal tender at midnight on 28 January 2002. The euro, which is divided into 100 cents, has a fixed exchange rate of just over 2 guilders.

The convenience of the euro means you no longer have to change money when travelling between member states. You can buy traveller's cheques in euros from UK banks and change them in Amsterdam in the same way as sterling traveller's cheques, although you will be charged a handling fee. Credit and debit cards work normally and your account will be debited by the sterling equivalent of the euro on your transactions slip. You should make sure you retain your transactions slip to compare with your account

Renting a car

Unless you're intending to tour the country around Amsterdam, a car will just be a source of problems. There are very few hotels with a free car park and you'll spend a fortune on parking meters (€2.27 per hour) if you want to avoid getting your car clamped. The city is comparatively small and public transport runs all night so you're really better off leaving the car at home. However, if you can't bear to be without your own wheels and are at least 21 years old, you'll be better off renting a car.. You can arrange this from home, otherwise the car rental offices at Schiphol (open from 6am to 11pm) are in Schiphol Plaza in the Arrivals lounge, before customs.

Europcar offers the best weekend rates (€335.80 for an Opel Corsa).
☎ 312 0316 4190 (Amsterdam)
www.europcar.com.

statement, to ensure that the currency conversion was correct.

There are plenty of cash machines in the city and at the airport, and you can easily withdraw cash using a credit or bankers card. If you need to carry large sums of money around with you, it's better to take traveller's cheques as pickpocketing is known to be rife in the city.

All major credit cards are recognised in the Netherlands and most large shops and restaurants will take cards as payment. Cash is still the general rule however, and you should ensure that you're not caught short without enough notes to cover your daily expenses. Car rental agencies will usually wish to see a credit card. Some shops will charge a 5% surcharge on credit card payments. Travellers resident in non-EU countries can claim back the value added tax (BTW) if they spend above a certain amount in a single visit to a shop. Check with customs, or look out for shops advertising tax-free shopping for tourists.

Budgeting

Life in Amsterdam can be expensive. You should expect to pay from €25 for a meal, from €3 for museum entry, from €5 for a coffee or a beer, €20-50 for entry to a nightclub or ticket for the theatre or a concert. After paying for your room and transport, you should allow at least €200 spending money. Of course, if you're travelling on a student budget, Amsterdam is still very much within your reach: you can get something to eat and a place to stay for very little, although the conditions can only be described as somewhat spartan. But however much you have to spend, the enormous choice of hotels and restaurants means that you'll always be able to find a room and a meal to suit your wallet.

Taking care of your health

If you're following a special course of medical treatment, make sure you take enough medication with you to cover the time you'll be away, as you can't be sure of finding it in Amsterdam.

EU citizens are entitled to free medical assistance (covering the cost of treatment and medication), from doctors approved by the A.N.O.Z. (Algemeen Nederlands Onderling Ziekenfonds), on presentation of an E111 form, which can be obtained in advance of travel from UK post offices.

You may be surprised to see many very well-stocked chemist's shops in Amsterdam selling everything from toothpaste and hair-care products to sun-screen, vitamins, food supplements and some medicinal items that you might normally only expect to obtain on prescription back home.

Things to look for in Amsterdam

Amsterdam is a city of diamonds, antiques, books and curiosities, so if you're looking to buy any of these, you'll find there are some very good bargains to be had. Many gadgets, items for the home, off-the-peg clothes and accessories are attractively priced and you'll often find items here that you can't get elsewhere. Generally speaking, Dutch fashions tend to follow the broad trends of other European countries and you'll find jersey, vinyl and other synthetic materials rather than natural linens and raw silk.

Formalities

Nationals of countries in the European Union, including children under 16, must have a valid identity card or passport. A passport that has expired within the last five years is also acceptable. If you're travelling from the USA, Canada, Australia or New Zealand you will require a valid passport. You will only require a visa if you are staying for three months or longer.

Insurance

The fixed insurance deals offered by tour operators usually include cover for cancellation or lost or stolen luggage. Provided you pay for your plane or train ticket by credit card, you're usually entitled to good cover for medical expenses and the cost of repatriation, but do check the extent of the cover offered with your credit card company before you go. If you make the bookings yourself, it's always a good idea to take out cover for the cost of repatriation with an accredited insurance company.

Local time

Amsterdam is one hour ahead of Greenwich Mean Time, 6 hours ahead of the U.S.A and Canada (Eastern Standard Time), 8 hours behind Australia (East Coast) and 10 hours behind New Zealand.

Voltage

In the Netherlands the current is 220 volts. It's handy to bring an adaptor, therefore, as they use two-pin plugs and sockets, not three.

Queen's Day

If you're planning to go to Amsterdam at the end of April, you'll need to book your hotel a long way in advance. 30 April is Queen's Day (see p. 33), when every town in the Netherlands is buzzing and people fill the streets to celebrate the queen's birthday. The actual festivities take place either the weekend before or after 30 April.

Useful source

Netherlands Tourist Office (VVV)

The VVV, the national tourist organisation, has three offices in Amsterdam and is the most reliable place to find information about accommodation, events and excursions (see page 35).

If you want to find out information before you leave home, the NBT (Netherlands Board of Tourism) has several offices abroad.

UK ☎ 0906 871 7777
USA ☎ 312 819 0300
Canada ☎ 416 363 1557

You can also check what will be going on when you get there by looking on NBT's website, www.visitholland.com.

Reflections of the Golden Age

In the 17th century Amsterdam became one of Europe's most flourishing capitals, thanks to the success of its traders and the freedom of thought permitted in the city. The Dutch welcomed exiles from all sides and in ten years the city had doubled in size. Meanwhile, the wealthy merchants of the prestigious Dutch East India Company were challenging the Portuguese monopoly of the spice trade.

▲ *John Calvin, 16th century wood engraving.*

The Calvinist creed

'Let us take the gain that comes to us as though it were from the hand of God.' With advice like that John Calvin was bound to appeal to the merchants of Amsterdam, who abandoned the teachings of the Spanish Catholics and welcomed many refugees, guaranteeing them both economic freedom and the freedom to think and worship as they chose.

Economic and religious liberalism

The vast influx of foreign capital made it possible to fund major maritime expeditions and also to develop local industries, such as brewing, silk-manufacture, diamond-cutting, printing, map-making and ship-building.

'In this great city where, other than myself, there is not a single man who is not engaged in trading goods, everyone is so occupied attending to his profit that I could stay here for the rest of my life without ever being seen by anyone.'
René Descartes, 1631.

A city without palaces

The only aim the rich Calvinists had in making money was to hoard their wealth. They were not interested in ostentatious splendour, or palaces, so there's no architecture worthy of the Golden Age. All you'll find are a few decorative masks

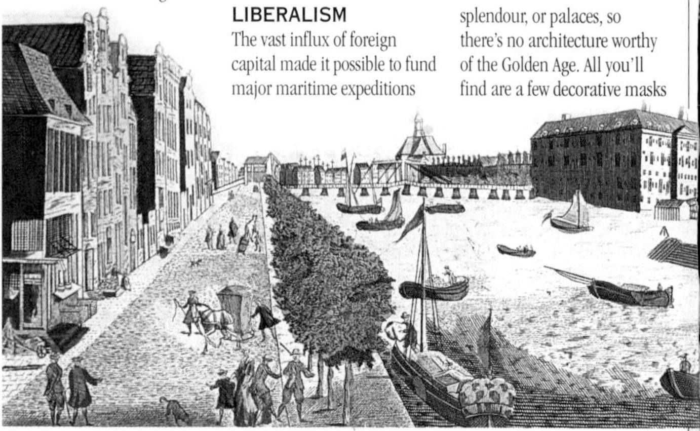

Frans Hals: *The Archers' Banquet*

and grotesque figures to enliven the modest gabled brick façades. Given that tax was assessed by the *'kavel'*, or plot of building land with a width of 7.35m/8yds and a depth of 60m/65yds, few people risked building on much larger plots.

EARLY TOWN PLANNING

To house a population that had tripled in forty years, it was decided to enlarge the city by digging three new canals, the Herengracht, the Keizersgracht and the Prinsengracht, around the port and the old quarters. The city was built all in one go and owes its harmonious quality to the rules imposed by the local council, which specified not only what materials could be used and the dimensions of the houses, but also located their inhabitants according to their social status, work or origins.

THE BIRTH OF BOURGEOIS ART

Freed from the yoke of religion, Dutch painters diversified into genres which reveal the material concerns of their wealthy bourgeois patrons. Commissions for single and group portraits came flooding into the studios of well-known painters such as Rembrandt and Frans Hals. Pictures of

Gerrit Dou: *Woman with Dropsy*

landscapes or simple church interiors were successful in a way unheard-of elsewhere. However these highly realistic depictions express a strict protestant morality – tavern scenes portray the evils of the excessive consumption of alcohol and tobacco, while the withered flowers of the still lifes are reminders of the vanity of worldly wealth and pleasures.

A DIFFERENT IMAGE OF REMBRANDT

Rembrandt van Rijn's real name was *Rembrandt Harmenszoon*, which means 'Rembrandt, son of Harmen'. He married in 1634, but then took his children's nanny as his mistress. However, in 1649 she left him and took him to court for breaking his promise to marry her. The painter then took on a young serving girl, Hendrickje Stoffels, who became his companion. However his behaviour was considered scandalous because Rembrandt's fame was such that he was regarded as a public figure. The Dutch Reformed Church condemned and reprimanded him and the unfortunate Hendrickje was banned from taking Holy Communion. The puritanical public turned against the artist, who later died in disgrace.

THE SEEDS OF MODERNISM

Turning its back on the floral exuberance of Art Nouveau, which was all the rage in France and Belgium, the Netherlands favoured a more rational form of architecture, which exploited the potential of emerging industrial techniques. The priority in Amsterdam, as in other places, was to use objects and furniture as a way of bringing art into daily life. In this way the modern look came into being.

THE NEW AESTHETIC CREED

The 'Arts and Crafts' exhibition held in London in 1880 marked the dawn of a new aesthetics which was to have an important influence on Dutch artists, particularly since the Netherlands' Germanic culture tends to favour severity over excess. The cult of the pure line and geometrical shapes acted as the vehicle of a new art form which gradually evolved towards Expressionism.

FUNCTIONALISM

H. P. Berlage was an important figure of the avant garde due to the way he exploited the qualities of old and new materials in functional ways. His monumental building for the Amsterdam stock exchange (1898-1903), consisted of a simple, sober structure of glass and steel, without any form of ornamentation, standing on a structure made from brick and stone.

THE AMSTERDAM SCHOOL

The socialist city council built affordable housing in south Amsterdam for the new working class. Rationalism and progress were the watchwords. However, the 'Dageraad' complex, designed between 1921 and 1923 by Michael de Klerk and P. L. Kramer, seems more fantastical than rational in conception. Expressionist ideas of movement are rather playfully reflected in the undulations, abrupt vertical constructions and the interplay of different colours.

THE DE STIJL MOVEMENT

Founded in Leiden in 1917 by Theo van Doesburg, the De Stijl movement, whose best representative is Piet Mondrian,

Robert Dusarduyn

Molsteeg, 5 and 7
☎ 623 21 89
Open Fri. 12.30-7pm and Sat. 11.30am-6pm or by appointment.

This former theatre designer, has specialised in collecting Art Deco objects and furniture since 1972. His collection of velvets from the Amsterdam School is well worth a look.

evolved out of neo-Plasticism. This was a theory of painting characterised by the rigorous use of very simple means of expression, such as horizontal and vertical lines, in combination with evenly-applied primary colours. Sometimes black and white would also be included, either as pure colours or mixed.

A pioneer of abstract art

Mondrian, whose early influences were Toorop and Seurat, is regarded as one of the pioneers of abstract art.He made a profound impression on all of contemporary western art, both through his pictures (*Composition in red, yellow and blue* and *Victory Boogie-Woogie*, among others) and his writings, such as the *De Stijl Manifesto*, *The Triptych of Evolution* or *Natural Reality and Abstract Reality*.

Modernism and daily life

The rigorously orthogonal forms he gave to his creations link Gerrit Rietveld (1888-1964) firmly to the De Stijl movement. The famous red and blue armchair, which he designed in 1919, marks the beginning of the era of simple furniture which could be mass-produced. Later he developed ever-more purified forms, which have influenced the work of many of today's designers.

Art Deco

This catch-all term, first used during the 1925 Paris International Exhibition, covers the very varied artistic production of the first half of the 20th century.

The furniture and objects made from 1915 onwards reflect a return to styles from the past, with massive forms, contrasting colours, geometrical decoration and the use of glass and steel. The use of rare materials (lacquer, skin, ivory) made this a luxury

style of limited production. The category of Art Deco covers both Rietveld's Cubist table and the comfortable 'Vanity Fair' armchair.

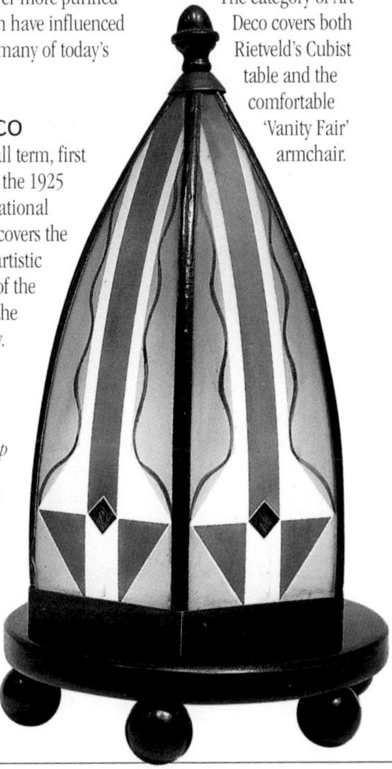

Art Deco lamp at Robert Dusarduyn's gallery

Liberty and Libertines

Since the 17th century, Amsterdam has been known for its tolerance. Though their apparently lax attitudes have often been criticised by their European neighbours, the Dutch uphold the right to true freedom of action and thought. In the Netherlands differences are accepted, whether a person is foreign, or homosexual, drops out of society or rejects moral conventions. Holland was also first to legalise abortion, allow euthanasia and decriminalise soft drugs.

Squatting, an Outdated Phenomenon

In the early 1970s it was fairly easy for a student to find free accommodation in a magnificent residence on the Herengracht. The *provos*' (see right) action to combat property speculation was more or less permitted by the city council, which preferred to see such buildings occupied before renovation. In what can only be seen as a sign of the times, the new housing law passed in 1986 put an end to this practice.

The *Provos*, Gentle Activists

In 1964 a group of young protesters describing themselves as non-violent ecologists campaigning against the status quo launched a series of amusing stunts known as 'happenings'. They met at the Dam and advocated non-polluting cars, the right to social housing and sexual freedom. These gentle subversives succeeded in getting elected on to Amsterdam's city council, where they instigated the anti-car policies in force today.

Coffee-Shops and Cannabis

The cannabis culture in the Netherlands was set in motion

by Kees Hockert, who, in 1961, discovered a loophole in Dutch law that made it illegal to possess dried cannabis flowers but not to grow them. Although the possession of soft drugs is still a crime in the Netherlands, the Dutch government permits the sale of cannabis resin in Amsterdam's three hundred or so coffee-shops. However the amount allowed for sale was recently reduced from 30gm (approximately 1oz) to 5gm (approximately 0.2oz).

A COUNTRY THAT WELCOMES FOREIGNERS

A quarter of the population is non-native and a hundred and forty-five nationalities live side-by-side in Amsterdam. Most are from Surinam, descendants of the black African slaves who were 'imported' to the Guyanas. In response to their desire to settle permanently in the Netherlands, an office was set up to help them to integrate into Dutch society.

'In what other country can one enjoy such complete freedom, can one sleep with fewer worries?'
René Descartes, 1631.

BUSINESS AND THE LIMITS OF PERMISSIVENESS

Recently the council of Delfzijl, a small town on the northern coast of the Netherlands, not far from Groningen, closed down all the local coffee-shops and opened a new one, which is run by a council employee. Not a bad way to keep a discreet eye on the customers and help balance the budget!

LOVE IN A SHOP WINDOW

Like any other port, Amsterdam has its prostitutes. The difference is that here there's none of the hypocrisy to be found in other countries – the prostitutes are on display in shop windows. Brothels are officially licensed and these ladies of easy virtue pay tax. In the final analysis it's a natural way of recognising their profession – which is, after all, the oldest in the world – and preventing them from touting for business on the streets, a practice which is still illegal in the country.

GAY CITY

After San Francisco, Amsterdam is the city with the highest number of gay clubs and bars in the world. It's one of the few countries in Europe where homosexual couples can marry and where they have the right to raise children. The gay community has a newspaper called the *Gay Krant*, and a centre for the protection of its rights. It also has an official 'pink day' in the holiday calendar.

Pottery

Among the precious cargoes brought back from the east by the ships of the Dutch East India Company was the famous blue-and-white porcelain from China. The first auction in 1604 caused enormous excitement among the Dutch bourgeoisie, whose dream it was to own such things. Chinese porcelain was expensive because of its rarity and was soon copied in the factories of Delft, which doubled in number between 1651 and 1665.

A technique from Italy

The use of faience was introduced to the Netherlands in the early 16th century by Italian potters who had established workshops in Antwerp. At this time kitchen equipment for daily use was made either of tin, wood or skin, following Germanic tradition. Politico-religious conflicts drove the Italian potters to migrate to the northern provinces, where they founded factories in Delft, Makkum, The Hague and Haarlem.

Delft faience

The terms porcelain and faience are often confused. In fact, although the factories of Delft and Makkum began to concentrate on producing copies of Chinese porcelain in

1613, Dutch factories have never made anything but white faience, decorated either in monochrome blue or a combination of colours. White Delftware pieces intended for kitchen use haven't been made for a very long time and are highly sought-after.

Porcelain or faience?

In porcelain fired at high temperatures (1,350°C/2,880°F), the china clay (kaolin) and the glaze form a highly resistant amalgam without flaws. Whilst porcelain is very thin and translucent, faience is made from a different kind of clay and is fired twice. After the first firing the earthenware object is covered in an opaque, white, tin-based enamel, and may be decorated. The piece is then fired again at 800°C. Faience is less solid than

HOW TO RECOGNISE REAL DELFTWARE

Beware! Not all blue-and-white ceramics are Delftware. Some souvenir-sellers have no scruples in inscribing the bottom of cheap imported ceramics with the royal crown and the magic words *Köninklijk Delftsblauw*. The first clue to the authenticity of your piece is the price. To be certain, however, you should make sure that you buy your Delftware from specialist shops, particularly if you're looking for antique pieces, and always check that they have the proper mark.

porcelain and may also have flaws, such as bubbles caused by firing at too high a temperature or the seeping of the decoration into the enamel. Delft faience has a second coating (transparent glaze) which heightens the colours. And in case you were wondering, the word 'faience' comes from the name of the Italian town of Faenza, where this technique was developed in the 15th century.

MAKKUM FAIENCE

Though less well-known by the general public, the royal factory at Makkum is the oldest in the Netherlands. It was founded in 1594 and since 1674 has been owned by the same family, the Tichelaars, who, from generation to generation, have passed down the secrets of the enamels that give the factory pieces their particular beauty. The blue monochrome or multi-coloured decoration is

always hand-painted by skilled craftspeople and is more delicate than that of Delft.

DE PORCELEYNE FLES

Most of the Delft factories closed their doors around 1742 as a result of competition from English and French products. The only factory to have maintained continuous production since it was founded in 1653 is the 'De Porceleyne Fles' factory. King Willem III gave it the title of royal factory in order to stimulate its declining output. Today, this and the Makkum factory are the only ones to produce real Delftware, which is authenticated by a mark on the underside of the object.

HOLLAND'S NATIONAL EMBLEM, THE TULIP

From the end of April, for eight or nine weeks, the polder between Leiden and Haarlem is transformed into a multicoloured carpet by its 8,000 hectares/20,000 acres planted with tulips. This wild flower from the steppes of central Asia, which first bloomed in Holland in 1594, aroused such a passion that growers have continued to modify its shapes and colours to this day.

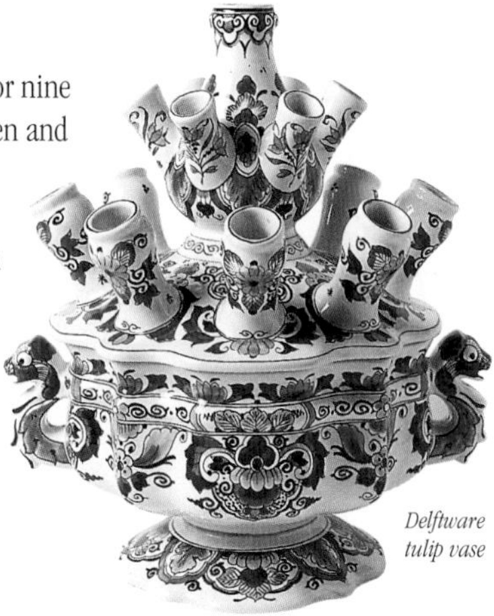

Delftware tulip vase

FLOWER OF SULTANS

In the 16th century Ferdinand I of Austria's ambassador to the court of the Ottoman sultan was surprised at the general passion for a flower then unknown in Europe – the tulip. He brought back a few bulbs, which were planted in the Imperial gardens in Vienna in 1554. Although the Turkish word for tulip is *'lale'*, the ambassador misunderstood his interpretor's description of the flower as resembling a turban (*tulband*), and thought this was in fact its name. In Latin it became known as *tulipa*.

THE TAMING OF THE TULIP

A French botanist, Charles de Lécluse, who was interested in the form and structure of the tulip, discovered its fantastic capacity for hybridisation. He created the first blooms of *Tulipa gesneriana* in the Leiden botanical gardens in 1594. Little did he realise, when he made his research public, that he was unleashing a kind of madness that was to seize hold of the entire Dutch nation.

Tulips in Art

The tulip, precious as a silver dish or a cut-crystal glass, became an element in the composition of still lifes. The Flemish painter Jan Breughel (1568-1625) was the first to depict it in all its ephemeral splendour. The Delft potters dedicated a special vase to the tulip, specifically designed to show off all its beauty to the greatest effect.

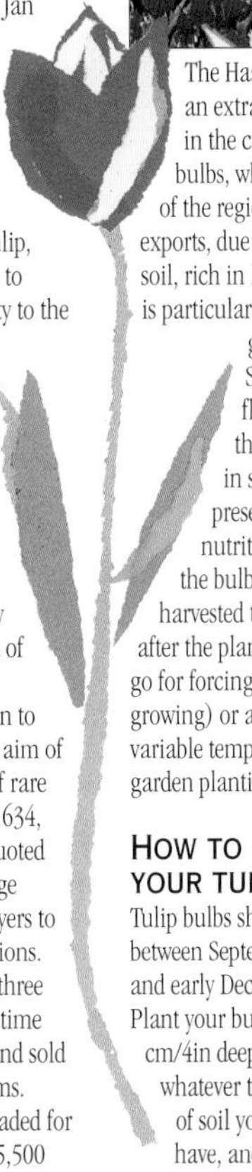

Tulipomania

The tulip's great success as a curiosity stimulated the greed of the speculators. All kinds of people began to experiment with the aim of obtaining a flower of rare shape or colour. In 1634, the tulip was even quoted on the stock exchange and had its own lawyers to take care of transactions. The craze lasted for three years, during which time tulips were bought and sold for astronomical sums. *Semper Augustus* traded for between 4 ,000 and 5,500 Florins. All this speculation came to an end when the market crashed, though the tulip remained a luxury item for a very long time afterwards.

Bulb Cultivation

The Haarlem region saw an extraordinary boom in the cultivation of bulbs, which became one of the region's main exports, due to its sandy soil, rich in limestone, which is particularly suited to growing tulips. Shortly after flowering the blooms are cut in such a way as to preserve the nutritional reserves of the bulb. These are harvested three months after the plant is cut back and go for forcing (greenhouse growing) or are stored at a variable temperature for garden planting.

How to Grow Your Tulip

Tulip bulbs should be planted between September and early December Plant your bulbs 10 cm/4in deep, whatever type of soil you have, and leave a space between them measuring roughly 15-20cm (5-7in). Depending on their variety and size, your tulips will bloom either in March or April (for early varieties) or May (for later varieties). The earth around the bulbs should be kept damp except when there's a frost.

Cultivars

Starting from the hundred or so tulip species to be found growing wild in central Asia, horticulturalists have developed around 900 tulip varieties, or cultivars. These fall into three categories, early, mid-season or late, according to the period in the year when they flower.

TOBACCO MANIA

In the 16th century a new craze hit Europe: the sniffing or smoking of the leaves of a plant discovered by Christopher Columbus among the American Indians. This luxury product, precious and rare, couldn't fail to interest the Dutch speculators, who set about acclimatising the plant in their colonies in Asia.

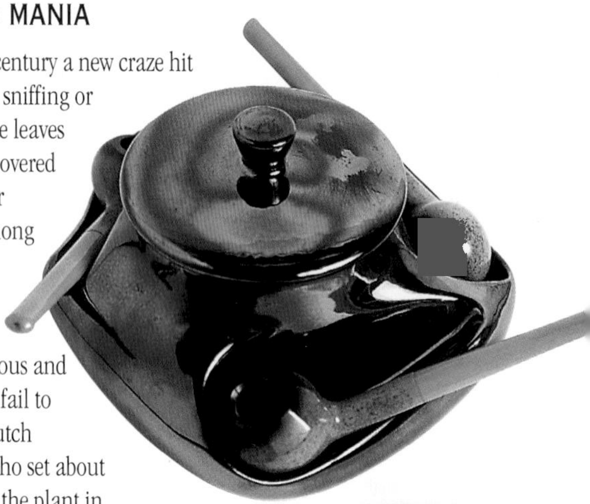

TOBACCO – BY ROYAL APPOINTMENT

Tobacco was cultivated intensively in Haiti by the Spanish and was at first prized for its medicinal qualities. It was ground to a fine powder and sniffed to cure headaches and drunk as a decoction to treat ulcers. The consumption of tobacco through smoking was a novelty introduced to the English court of Elizabeth I by Sir Walter Raleigh, who was a keen pipe-smoker.

NICOTIANA TABACUM

Although the use of tobacco was introduced to the Netherlands by English soldiers, it was the merchants of the East India Company who acclimatised this American plant to Asia and South Africa. In the 18th century tobacco was regarded as a luxury and was included as a special privilege in the rations given to the officers and seamen of the East India Company.

THE FAMOUS PIPES OF GOUDA

The vogue for tobacco led to the birth of a new industry – the manufacture of earthenware pipes. The first factories appeared in the Netherlands around 1610, when the pipe-makers of Gouda were considered to be the best. Each factory put its own mark on the stem of the pipe and twenty-five different marks have been identified on porcelain pipes made in Gouda.

THE TASTE OF TOBACCO

Although there are a great many varieties of tobacco, with different tastes, smells and burning qualities, it's only after two final processes, 'saucing' and 'flavouring' that they come into their own. Saucing involves flavouring the leaves

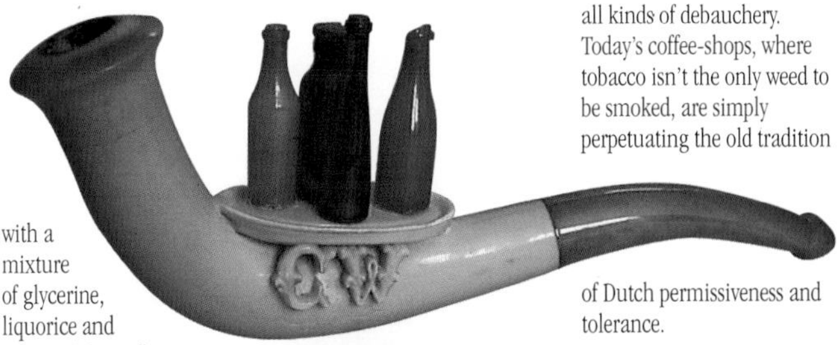

with a mixture of glycerine, liquorice and sugar, whilst in flavouring they're treated with various essences, such as rum or orange.

THE MYSTERY PIPE

Between 1900 and 1940 a new pipe, known as the mystery pipe or *door-roker*, was all the rage. An image would appear under the glaze as the pipe was smoked. The secret lay in the stamping of a design on the highly porous clay before the glaze was fired, which would then be coloured by the nicotine.

SMOKING OR NON SMOKING?

Unlike many other western societies, the Netherlands hasn't yet adopted policies to restrict consumption of tobacco and cigarettes. In restaurants and cafés there are few non-smoking zones, and as a result you may find it difficult to breathe when first entering some of the coffee houses. However, tobacco and the smell of smoke are an integral part of the ambiance. In the 17th century Dutch painters even created a new genre, paintings of interiors with smokers, of which Adrian Brouwer was the most famous exponent. In these smoky dens customers who hadn't yet collapsed in a state of drunkeness, would indulge in all kinds of debauchery. Today's coffee-shops, where tobacco isn't the only weed to be smoked, are simply perpetuating the old tradition of Dutch permissiveness and tolerance.

Adrian Brouwer:
Interior with tobacco smokers

SMOKIANA

Prinsengracht, 488
☎ 421 17 79
Open Wed.-Sat. noon-6pm, or by appt Mon. and Tue.

Meerschaums, ethnic pipes from all over the world, pipes made from wood, earthenware or porcelain, snuffboxes, cigar and opium boxes, hookahs and opium pipes – a paradise for lovers of smoking paraphernalia.

AMSTERDAM, A CITY OF CIGARS

Amsterdam is the most important market in the world for the sale of wrappers, the leaves in which cigars are rolled, which originate in Indonesia. The city is also famous for its cigars, their subtle aroma obtained by mixing between fifteen and twenty different kinds of tobacco from Java, Sumatra, Havana, Brazil, etc.

Delicious Dutch cheese

For many people Dutch cheese means either Edam or Gouda. Yet Holland produces many different kinds of cheese and is the top cheese-exporter in the world. It was in the Middle Ages that the Dutch began to specialise in the manufacture of pressed 'uncooked' cheese. Their unique flavour comes from their capacity to age well and the addition of spices from the Moluccas. Dutch cheese can be left to mature and tasted like wine, from the soft, fruity young cheeses to the spicy dryness of the older varieties.

How the cheese is made

Apart from a small amount of goat's cheese *(geitenkaas)*, most cheese in Holland is made from cow's milk. Dutch cows are among the best milk-producers in the world. Each individual animal can produce up to 6,136 litres/1,350 gallons a year. The milk is made to curdle by adding a fermenting agent and rennet. The whey is then separated from the curd by a process of stirring, and the curd is put into a mould. After it has been pressed the cheese is immersed in brine for several days. The flavour and texture of the cheese, which ages as it dries, depends on the length of time it's left to mature.

Cheese from the south...

Make sure you taste some of the delicious farm cheeses while you're in Amsterdam. They're famous for their complex flavours, which grow stronger as they age. Gouda comes in wide, flat rounds and can be eaten *jong* (three to six months old), *pittig* (eighteen months old), *oud* (two years old) or *heel oud* (two and a half years old or more). The older the cheese, the fuller the flavour. Mature Gouda tastes a bit like parmesan. It also comes in a miniature variety, called Amsterdammer, which is always eaten young.

... and the north

Edam is the characteristic little round cheese whose deep

Words every cheese-lover should know

Kaas: cheese
Boerenkaas: farm cheese made with unpasturised milk. To make sure it's the real thing, look for the special seal stamped on the crust.
Jong: young
Belegen: medium-mature
Pittig: full-flavoured
Oud: mature
Heel oud: extra-mature

yellow crust is covered in a layer of red wax for export. It's dryer than Gouda and can also be eaten at different stages: *jong*, *belegen* (one year old) and *oud* (two years old). Mimolette is another widely-exported northern cheese. Its name means 'half-soft' and comes from its consistency, which it loses as it ages.

The Gouda nouveau has arrived!

Gouda is made using milk flavoured with fresh herbs and, like wine, arrives in the shops at particular times of year. The soft, delicate May Gouda *(meikaas)* is around for only six weeks, from mid-June to the end of July and the Dutch celebrate its arrival, as they do that of the herring.

You can tell *Leidse kaas*, which is flavoured with cumin seeds, from Gouda by the famous crossed keys of the city of Leiden printed on its orange-coloured rind. Friesland also produces a cheese flavoured with cloves, called *Friese Nagel kaas*.

Cheese markets

The biggest cheese market in the Netherlands is held in Alkmaar in north Holland on Friday mornings from May to October. Closer to Amsterdam (30km/20 miles) is the town of Edam itself, whose very picturesque market is held on Wednesdays in July and August 10am-12.30pm. Here the cheeses are weighed, under the eye of a bowler-hatted inspector.

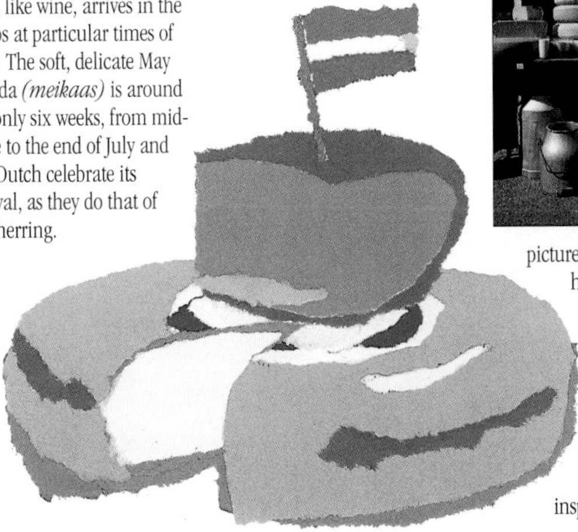

Buying cheese

Here's where to find the best mature Dutch farm cheeses, to buy or just taste.

De Franse Kaasmakers
Marnixstraat, 192
☎ 626 22 10
Tue.-Thu. 10am-6pm, Fri. 9am-6pm, Sat. 9am-5pm.

Kaashahandel Arxhoek Wout
Damstraat, 19
☎ 622 91 18
Mon.-Fri. 9am-6pm, Sat. 9am-5pm, Sun. noon-4pm.

Amsterdamse Kaashal
Lijnbaansgracht, 32
Fri. 9am-6pm, Sat. 9am-4pm.

When you're in Amsterdam make sure you visit the market in Albert Cuypstraat (open daily, including Sat.) or the Saturday market in Noordermarkt (see p.54).

DIAMONDS ARE FOREVER

A jeweller in Antwerp cut the first faceted diamond in 1475. The full splendour of these hard stones can only be appreciated when they're cut in such a way that exploits the laws governing the refraction and reflection of light to the greatest possible extent. The diamond-cutting workshops of Amsterdam were established at the end of the 16th century and have produced some very famous diamonds, such as the Cullinan and the Kohinoor. The unrivalled skill of Amsterdam's diamond-cutters has turned the city into the diamond capital of the world.

THE FOUR 'C'S

Most of the diamonds cut in Amsterdam come from South Africa originally. They're bought in London, however, at sales called 'sights' which take place ten times a year. Diamonds are valued according to four criteria, which are known as the four 'c's. These are the cut, colour, clarity and carat – or weight – of the stone.

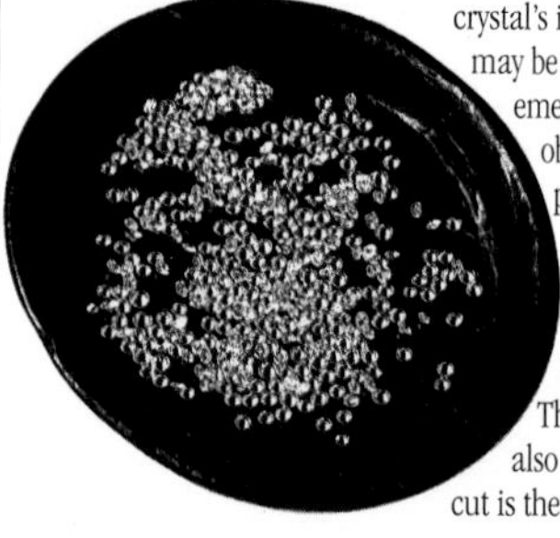

FROM PYRAMID TO BRILLIANT

Diamonds are made of carbon crystallised by the combined effects of high pressures and temperatures. In their uncut state they're eight-sided. When cut in half they fall into pyramids, the shape in which they were mounted as jewels in the days before the first rose-cut was invented. The different types of cut depend on the crystal's initial shape, which may be rectangular, emerald, baguette or oblong, marquise or pear-shaped.

THE DIAMOND'S SPARKLE

The most common, but also the most expensive cut is the 'brilliant'. This consists of a 'table' surrounded by 32 upper facets, which slope at an angle of 35° towards the 24 lower facets, themselves sloping at an angle of 41°. A total of 57 facets gives the greatest possible amount of coloured sparkle, the 'fire' of the diamond.

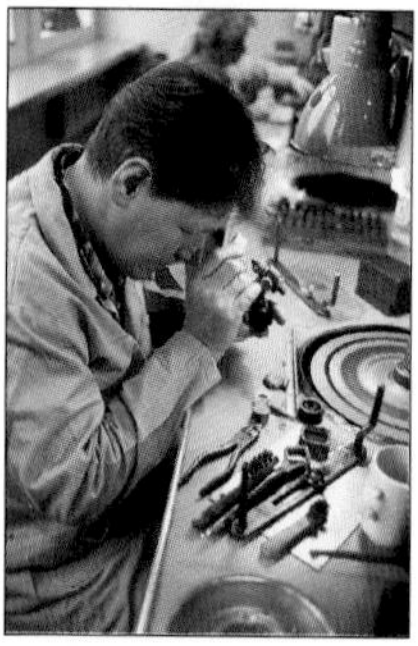

SUBTLE COLOURS

A yellowish hue is regarded as highly undesirable in a diamond. However, if, as a result of the presence of another mineral in the carbon at the time of crystallisation, a diamond is tinted a uniform pink, blue, green or black, this colour gives it an enhanced value.

PURITY AND BRILLIANCE

A high-quality diamond must be completely pure. The over-visible presence of other elements or peculiarities of crystallisation (clouds, flaws, or feathers) takes away much of its value. Diamonds are classified into seven categories according to a scale of imperfections that are visible to the naked eye (with the aid of a magnifying glass). These range from the flawless, the purest type, to the kind with the most imperfections, known as Piqué III.

COUNTING IN CARATS

These precious jewels are weighed in metric carats, one carat being equal to two hundred milligrams/0.007oz (5 carats = 1gm/0.04oz) or a hundred points. A 0.01-carat brilliant has exactly the same number of facets as one weighing 22 carats.

COMPETITIVE PRICES

Besides giving you a greater range of size and quality, buying a diamond in a diamond-cutting shop has the added advantage of being much cheaper than at home. Prices vary from €25,500 to €3,500 per carat, depending on the quality of the stone. So a diamond cut as an emerald costs less than a brilliant for the same number of carats, since less of the substance is lost. Yellowish coloration and the presence of small inclusions are also factors that make the price of a diamond more affordable.

REAL OR FAKE?

All the diamond-cutters in Amsterdam and all the major jewellers provide certificates of authenticity. These large businesses wouldn't want to undermine their reputations by selling a zircon as a diamond. Better still, they have English-speaking sales personnel who are ready to spend the necessary time with you, presenting an entire range of diamonds to suit both your heart and your wallet.

THE DIFFERENT SHAPES OF DIAMOND

- SQUARE PRINCESS
- BRILLIANT
- MARQUISE
- PEAR-SHAPED
- HEART-SHAPED
- PRINCESS
- OVAL
- EMERALD
- SQUARE
- BAGUETTE

The Art of Living in Amsterdam

To make up for the lack of housing in a city that has kept its organic structure almost intact since the 17th century, Amsterdammers have had to be both imaginative and practical. Pioneers of converting old buildings, they invented both lofts and houseboats. Another example of the city's unusual housing is the transformation of its former hospices or *hofjes*.

Loft Living

Back in the 1970s, the only place where could you get a reasonably-priced room in the centre of Amsterdam was on Prinseneiland and Prinsengracht, where the great number of abandoned workshops, disused warehouses and the odd empty church gave architects an enormous choice of spaces to convert as they chose, so long as they preserved the façade. Life without any walls, or conventional layouts, became the challenge for those inventing a non-conformist lifestyle.

Houseboats: Life on the Water

From old Rhine barges and rafts surmounted by little shacks, to craft that look as though they're going to sink any minute, the floating houses of Amsterdam first appeared on the city's canals in the 1950s, in response to the housing shortage. Originally inhabited by people on the fringes of society, they've become dream homes for the young and those strapped for cash, since a mooring costs only around €227 a year.

Keeping the Numbers Down

This type of housing was legalised in 1973 as a way of limiting the number of houseboats on the canals, which had a worrying tendency to multiply. Nowadays surveys suggest there's a fleet of 2,400 houseboats, of which only a thousand are licensed, although the others are not actually illegal. They're concentrated on Prinsengracht, Brouwersgracht and the

Amstel. Of course every houseboat is connected to the telephone and the city's supplies of electricity and running water.

HOFJES

Here and there in Jordaan you'll see signs pointing discreetly down narrow alleyways to a *hofje*. These

former hospices, which were originally intended as housing for elderly people in need, consist of tiny houses built round a little courtyard or garden. The *hofjes* have their devotees who, with a few modifications, manage to

create little islands of tranquillity for themselves in the bustling heart of the city.

SOME THINGS YOU NEED TO KNOW...

Pedestrians beware! In Amsterdam the bicycle reigns supreme. Don't even step on to a pavement without first checking whether or not it's a cycle track. If it is, a sharp 'ding-ding!' will soon remind you of the fact in no uncertain terms. And then, there's the question of punctuality. This is a city that runs on time. Don't think you can turn up to meet someone the usual fifteen minutes late. Hard work and simplicity are Calvinist virtues; but when the offices close at 5pm, the Dutch like to take some time to relax. After eating their evening meal between 6 and 6.30pm, they like to go on family bike rides, visit their friends or spend the evening in a favourite café.

COSY CORNER

It's hardly surprising, in a country where it's wet and windy for most of the year, that Amsterdammers' homes are places of comfort, carefully

furnished and decorated and filled with vases of flowers all year round. People here like to be comfortable and their houses tend to be fresh, tidy and impeccably clean, with that extra little something that reflects their own special decorative flair. As soon as the sun comes out, the pavements are covered in tables and chairs. This very particular lifestyle is known as *gezelligheid*, which means at once intimate, comfortable and sociable.

'BROWN CAFÉS' AND *KRANTCAFÉS*

Cafés have always been a kind of second home to the Dutch, who don't often invite people into their own homes. The decor of the traditional 'brown cafés', or *bruine kroegen*, is all nicotine-stained walls, dark wood panelling, sparkling copper pumps and sawdust on the floor. In complete contrast, the interiors of the big cafés are generally light, spacious, and designed with a resolutely contemporary feel. These cafés tend to have a younger clientele.

KRANTCAFÉ

The Amsterdammers' favourite pastime is sitting in a café for hours on end reading the newspaper, so it would be unthinkable not to find an enormous range of daily papers *(krant)* on offer in your favourite café. Some large cafés, such as the very trendy *De Jaren*, or the cosier *American Café*, even provide a large table with good lighting, where you can sit in comfort and read papers all day if you so desire. English-language newspapers are sometimes available too.

THE DAILY GRIND

After the departure of the office-workers, who come in for their lunch-time snack, the afternoon hours in the cafés are left to the cards and chess players. Aperitif time starts at around 5pm, while the *eetcafés*, where a portion of the dish of the day *(dagschotel)* tends to be generous and cheap, fill up with young people, who all eat sitting round one big table.

CONVIVIAL AND CHEERY

'Brown cafés' tend to be quiet during the day, but liven up in the evening, particularly on Friday and Saturday nights. Regulars and casual customers go there to talk in a free and easy atmosphere without any social pretence. Most drink beer or spirits, some sing songs, others discuss the latest match or set the world to rights with friends who were only strangers an hour ago.

DRINKERS' JARGON

When you order a beer you'll usually be given a draught lager that is brewed in

Amsterdam, either Heineken or Amstel. Try asking for a 20 or 25cl *pils* (about half a pint) or, for the very thirsty, a 50cl *vaas* (about a pint). In both cases the beer should be served with a head two inches thick. The Dutch sometimes drink beer with a little chaser of *jenever* (gin). This strange practice is known as *kopstoot,* or headbanging, no doubt because of the migraines it causes.

THE *PROEFLOKAAL*

Jenever, a spirit distilled from cereals and juniper berries, has its own places of worship, known as *proeflokalen* or tasting-houses. Here, the casks are lined up on the counter and you drink standing up, from a little glass filled to the brim, and you have to suck in the entire contents in one go, without losing a drop. *Jenever* is drunk either young *(jong)* or mellowed with age *(oud)* and is often served with salted herring.

REGULAR OR DECAF?

The Dutch love their coffee, so if you're planning to hang out in cafés all day, here are a few things you really ought to know. One cup of arabica coffee contains between 50 and 100mg of caffeine and the same quantity of robusta coffee contains between 120 and 150mg, while a cup of decaffeinated coffee only contains around 1 or 2mg. Drinking large quantities of coffee (more than nine cups a day) causes a rise in cholesterol levels of between 8 and 10%. A 100mg dose of caffeine stimulates the metabolism, and may increase your expenditure of energy and calories by 16% in two hours.

NON-SMOKERS, GIVE UP!

The tradition of tobacco smoking has been well-established in Amsterdam since the 17th century and isn't about to fade away. To be sure of this you only have to step inside a 'brown café' one evening, when the air is heavy with clouds of smoke. Non-smokers will almost certainly be happier sitting in one of the larger cafés, which sometimes have specially designated non-smoking areas.

DUTCH CUISINE

Although the Netherlands is not known for its gourmet cooking or haute cuisine, it does offer a wide selection of tasty food, and quantities are usually copious. Thanks to the city's varied immigrant communities, those with a taste for spicy food won't be disappointed. Dishes worth mentioning include the *rijsttafel,* which combines rice with many different Indonesian dishes and flavours.

THE FLAVOURS OF THE EAST

The first Dutch East India Company was founded in Amsterdam in 1594. From their voyages in the Far East, the Dutch brought back a huge quantity of spices, such as pepper, nutmeg, cloves, saffron and chillies, as well as a taste for Indonesian cuisine which has found its way into Dutch cooking.

THE *RIJSTTAFEL*

The *rijsttafel* is a dish with a gargantuan selection of Indonesian flavours. It is usually made up of rice, accompanied by around eight (although it can rise to as many as fifty) different dishes, including such delicacies as deep fried prawns, chicken kebabs or meatballs with steamed vegetables. This meal is now so much a part of Dutch heritage that the Delft factories have created a specially-designed *rijsttafel* dinner service, with nine different plates that fit together around a central star-shaped dish.

TRADITIONAL DUTCH COOKING

For simple, nourishing Dutch food look out for restaurants displaying the *Neerlands Dis*

sign. Here you can be sure of finding a hearty meal, including such traditional specialities as split-pea soup flavoured with ham, so thick that you can stand a spoon up in it! For a starter try the *bitterballen,* delicious deep fried meat balls from which little clouds of steam escape as you break their crisp breadcrumb crust.

Hutspot

This traditional dish of meat stew with seasonal vegetables, commemorates the liberation of Leiden, which was besieged by the Spanish in 1574. Legend has it that after the enemy had abandoned their positions, a young boy found a pot of stew which had been left behind and used it to feed the town's starving inhabitants. Although today's ingredients may not be entirely authentic, as the potatoes it invariably contains had not yet found their way on to European tables, it is still recognised as a traditional dish that the people of Leiden consume each year on 3 October.

How to eat a herring

To eat a *nieuwe haring* the same way as the Dutch, tip your head back, hold your herring by its tail and dangle it into your mouth, then gulp it down in a few bites! New herrings should smell of the sea and have no dark red patches on their backs. Wash it down with a glass of iced *jenever*.

Seafood, a popular choice

The herring fishing season begins on 25 May. The Dutch are great fans of the humble herring and like to eat it raw, seasoned with peppercorns *(nieuwe haring)*. A great many *haringkar* (herring stands) are stationed along the canals all year round, serving *maatsjesharing,* or marinated herrings with onions. Another popular choice for many Dutch people are eels caught in the IJsselmeer *(paling)*, which may be eaten 'green' or smoked.

Coffee breaks

Although the Dutch don't spend much time over their meals, coffee breaks are sacred. *Kopjes koffie* are consumed all day long, usually accompanied by something sweet, such as delicious Droste chocolate pastilles or biscuits flavoured with ginger *(speculaas)* or butter. You'll find your will-power crumbling away when faced with a tempting fruit tart or *Limburgse vlaai*, which comes in over twenty different, mouth-watering varieties.

Festivals in Amsterdam

Sinterklaas (St Nicholas's Day) and *Koninginnedag* (Queen's Day) are celebrated throughout the Netherlands, but nowhere more strongly than in Amsterdam. Unlike most other European countries, the Netherlands celebrates St Nicholas's Day on 5 rather than 6 December, and it's an occasion for family and friends to get together and have fun. On 30 April Amsterdam celebrates Queen's Day with an impressive programme of events which attracts over 500,000 people each year.

Patron saint of Amsterdam

St Nicholas really did exist. Bishop of Myra, he lived from 271 to around 343 AD and was renowned for performing such miracles as calming stormy seas, saving boats from shipwreck, rescuing children from the butcher's knife and putting dowries in the boots of poor young girls. The patron saint of sailors, merchants and children, it was only natural that Amsterdam should be placed under his protection.

Once upon a time...

Today St Nicholas is the benefactor of all children and the Dutch believe he lives in Spain, where he writes down everything children do in a big red book, while Black Pete, his faithful helper, gets the presents ready for the end of the year. St Nicholas, dressed in red with a long white beard, rides a white horse, while Black Pete carries a big sack of toys over his shoulder.

A celebration for young and old

Children are generally well behaved at this time of year, as they know St Nicholas can hear their voices through the chimney. Each night, hoping he will come, they put carrots and hay inside their shoes for his horse. When the great day arrives, Black Pete swaps them for a present or a sweet. Adults join in the fun as well and families, friends and colleagues give each other small gifts wrapped in an original style and accompanied by a poem or a riddle. These poems often make fun of the recipient, who has to read them aloud and guess what's inside the package.

Sweet St Nicholas

Four types of sweets, biscuits and cakes are traditionally eaten around *Sinterklaas*: *borstplaat* or fondant, *speculaas*, *letterbanket* and *kerstkrans*. *Borstplaat* is a sort of flat caramel sweet, made with butter or cream, and at this time of year *speculaas* biscuits are made in the shape of St Nicholas. *Letterbanket* is made from puff pastry and marzipan and party guests are each given one bearing the first letter of their name.

Kerstkrans are crown-shaped delicacies covered with glacé fruits, used to decorate the table, and eaten with relish afterwards!

KONINGINNEDAG

Koninginnedag, or Queen's Day, originated on 31 August 1898 on Queen Wilhelmina's 18th birthday. When Juliana succeeded her mother she proclaimed that the 'Day of the Queen' would be celebrated on her own birthday, 30 April. Her daughter Beatrix, the current reigning monarch, decided to keep the date as 30 April even though her birthday is actually 31 January. On *Koninginnedag* every town in Holland is decked out in orange, the Royal Family's colour.

MUSIC AND MARKET STALLS

On the night of 29 April, it's party time in Amsterdam, with singing, dancing and music, and quite a few beers to help things along, of course. Around two million people fill the streets, where actors put on plays, while acrobats amaze the crowds and Dam Square becomes one big funfair. The following day the big clean-up starts and the city turns into a huge flea market as every man, woman and child clears out their junk and sets it out on a stall in the street. On this one day, normal trading licences are suspended, so anyone can sell whatever they like. You're bound to come home with a bargain you never knew you wanted!

THE VONDELPARK

On Queen's Day, the Vondelpark is dedicated to children, although parents are encouraged to join in the fun and games. There are races, competitions, games, fishing challenges, and even obstacle courses for bikes with backwards handlebars!

WHERE TO FIND *SPECULAAS*

Around *Sinterklaas* the image of St Nicholas can be found on *speculaas* biscuits in bakeries all over Holland. They come in all shapes and sizes and look so good it's almost a shame to eat them. Here's a few places to seek them out:

Banketbakkerij Cornelius Arnold
van Baerlestraat, 93
☎ 662 12 28.

Beune Banketbakkerij
Haarlemmerdijk, 156
☎ 624 83 56.

Huis van Wely Sinds
Beethovenstraat, 72
☎ 662 20 09.

TAKE TO THE WATER!

Many people take out their motor boats, accompanied by friends and a full cargo of beer, of course, and go to listen to a concert or get together to sing, chat and have some fun. There are so many of these boats that navigation is not always easy and some canals become almost completely blocked, although the atmosphere is always friendly and good-natured.

Amsterdam

Practicalities

GETTING AROUND

Given that Amsterdam is comparatively small and difficult to get round in a car (and even harder to find a parking space), you're better off getting a detailed map of the city at the VVV (see p. 9) and do your exploring on foot, taking your bearings from the canals. Apart from Plantage and Pijp, the districts are arranged inside a ring of canals bordered by the Singelgracht. Allow two days to explore the main attractions, assuming you take a tram or boat every now and then to get you from one district to another. If the weather's good, the most pleasant way to get around quickly is to take a leaf out of the Amsterdammer's book and rent a cheap bicycle.

BY METRO, TRAM AND BUS

These run from 6am to midnight. After that, there's a night bus service.
The public transport network covers a wide area, and is quick, cheap and easy to use. There are 3 metro lines, 17 tram routes, 5 bus routes and 8 night bus routes covering the city centre and suburbs.

Most of the trams leaving from the central station pass through the Dam and Muntplein. For other stops, consult your map or ask the driver, who'll give you the information you need in English. The metro won't be much use to you unless you're going to east Amsterdam.
If you've hired a bike, though, remember there's nothing to stop you taking it on the metro with you.

Single tickets (€1.35) can be bought in the metro and from bus and tram drivers, but it's better value to buy a pass in advance. You can buy one lasting 24 hours (€5.45) or 2, 3 or 4 days, or you can buy a *strippenkaart* with 15 or 45 boxes that you have validated by the driver or by machine (you use two boxes per journey within the centre zone).
Once validated, it allows you to travel on different forms of transport for a period of 1 hour. The cards are on sale

in the GVB kiosk opposite the central station and in newsagents' or tobacco shops or from automatic ticket dispensers in the rail and metro stations. To get on or off the tram or metro, press the button marked '*deur open*'.

By bike

Bikes have a great many advantages: no parking problems, no hills, absolute priority over cars and pedestrians (who are given a mouthful if they dare set so much as a toe on the sacrosanct cycle lanes) and no worries about timetables. The only disadvantage is that you might find your vehicle has been stolen, as happens fairly often. So when hiring your bike, make sure it comes with a good lock. Rental gets cheaper the more days you take. Remember, though, that most of these bikes have only one gear and that you put the brakes on by pedalling backwards, which can take some getting used to. Bike hire offices are open seven days a week from 9am to 6pm.

When you hire a bike, you'll be asked for proof of identity and a deposit of around €23 or your credit card details.

Koenders Take-a-bike
Stationsplein, 12
☎ 624 83 91
You'll find the cheapest daily and weekly rates near the central station.

Mac Bike
Marnixstraat, 220
☎ 626 69 64
Rents out solid Dutch bikes at good rates.

Bike City
Bloemgracht, 68-70
☎ 626 37 21
This shop will provide you with route suggestions and anti-theft devices.

Yellow Bike
Nieuwezijds Kolk, 29.
☎ 620 69 40
Guided cycle tours through Amsterdam or the nearby countryside, conducted in English. Make sure you reserve in advance.

By taxi

There aren't many taxis in the city and they're expensive, so locals tend to use them mostly for journeys at night. You'll find taxi ranks outside the central station, on the Dam, Leidseplein, Rembrandtplein, Nieuwmarkt, Waterlooplein and Spui. The central telephone number is ☎ 677 77 77.

Although the classic taxi is little used in the city centre, you can get to your hotel quickly by watertaxi. Many hotels have special landing stages for just this reason. Watertaxis have a standard meter (about €1 a minute) and a radio telephone. The most luxurious of them can carry as many as 8 people ☎ 530 10 90.

By pedalo

You can hire a *canalbike* or two or four-seater pedalo at the piers near Leidseplein, between the Rijksmuseum and the Heineken brewery, opposite the Westerkerk and on Keizersgracht/Leidsestraat. There's a €136 deposit and they cost €4.75 per person per hour. You'll be given a canal map and ideas for routes and you can return your pedalo to any of the piers. Open May to October from 10am to 9pm (10.30pm in summer), and November to April from 10am to 6pm.

Canal Bike
Weteringschams, 24
☎ 626 55 74.

By boat

Travelling by *canalbus* is fun and very pleasant in summer. A shuttle service runs every 20 minutes (every 25-45 minutes in winter) between the central station and the Rijksmuseum from 10am to 8pm. There's a fixed charge of €12.50 for the day, which allows you to stop off whenever you like (they stop at Leidseplein, the intersection of Leidsestraat and Keizersgracht and Anne Frank's house on Prinsen-gracht. The whole journey takes about an hour. Tickets can be bought in hotels and *Canalbus* kiosks. Two-hour candlelit trips with wine and gouda tasting run on Friday and Saturday evenings, leaving from the Rijksmuseum at 9.30pm (☎ 623 98 86).

The *museumboot* service takes you on a complete tour of the city, starting from the central station and travelling along the loveliest canals before returning via the port. Boats leave every 30 mins (45 mins in winter) from 10am to 5pm, making six stops, enabling you to visit a museum or do some shopping. You can buy a ticket for the whole day (€12.50) or half a day (€10.20) from the VVV or at the Rederij Lovers kiosk opposite the central station (☎ 622 21 81). This will also get you a 10 to 50% reduction on your museum entrance fee. If you like the idea of a one-hour sight-seeing trip on a river boat, by day or night, there are a number of organisations running these every 15 mins from 6 to 10pm. You can leave from either the central station or the Rokin.

The best way to tour the canals in real style is to hire an elegant wooden saloon boat dating from 1920. The captain will see to your every need, you'll have access to the bar and you can even order a buffet if you so choose. This magnificent saloon boat holds a maximum of 12 people (*Salonboot 'Paradis'* ☎ 684 93 38).

CONTACTING HOME

To phone outside Holland, dial 00 followed by the country code, then the phone number. If you're calling Amsterdam from another town in the Netherlands, dial 020 before the seven digit number. Public telephone boxes are green and take coins or magnetic cards, which you can buy in post offices, stations, the VVV and newsagents' shops. Most also accept international credit cards. At the Telecenter (Raadhuistraat, 48), which is open day and night, you can pay either in cash or with a credit card or traveller's cheques. It's cheaper to call after 6.30pm or at weekends. Lastly, if you use the telephone in your hotel room, remember you'll be fairly heavily surcharged.

Dialling codes from the Netherlands:
UK ☎ 00 44
Ireland ☎ 00 353
USA and Canada ☎ 00 1
Australia ☎ 00 61
New Zealand ☎ 00 64

For internal direct enquiries call ☎ 06 8008 and for international enquiries call ☎ 06 0418.

You can buy stamps at any post office (open Mon.-Fri. 9am-6pm, Sat. until 1pm), or buy them together with your postcards from a tobacconist's or souvenir shop. Post letters going outside Holland in the slot marked '*overige postcodes*' in the red letterboxes.

BANKS AND BUREAUX DE CHANGE

Banks are open from 9am to 4 or 5pm Monday to Friday, with some open on Thursday evenings and Saturday mornings. All banks are closed on public holidays. GWK and post offices usually offer the most competitive exchange rates and the lowest commission, and the GWK branches at Schiphol airport and Centraal Station are open 24 hours. Bureaux de change can be found throughout the city centre. The rates are usually less competitive than banks, but commission can mount up. Thomas Cook and American Express don't charge commission for cashing their own traveller's cheques, but you may find the rates less

NO MERCY FOR CAR DRIVERS

The fact that you've got a foreign number plate won't mean a thing! If you've forgotten to pay for your parking space (€2.25 per hour from 9am-8pm except Sundays), you'll be disagreeably surprised to find your car immobilised by a clamp. It will cost you €59 to get it removed. So leave your car in a car park or buy an all-day parking permit (€12.95).

To have a clamp removed or to buy a parking permit: **Service Parkeerbeheer**, Bakkerstraat, 13 (or various addresses around the city). Open 24 hours.

competitive, and remember you'll still be charged a fee for cashing euro traveller's cheques into euros. You can always withdraw money using your credit or

debit card, either from an ATM or over the counter (see 'Cash and Budgeting'). You'll get the worst deal if you change money at your hotel or in tourist bureaux.

American Express: ☎ 625 09 22
GWK: Centraal Station ☎ 627 27 31
Thomas Cook: 23-25 Old Centre ☎ 625 09 22

Tourist offices

VVV
Stationplein, 10;
Leidseplein, 12;
Schiphol Plaza (airport)
☎ 00 31 900 400 4040
Email:.
info@amsterdamtourist.nl

As well as information leaflets and maps of the city and the surrounding area, you'll find English-speaking staff, who will provide details of hotels, forthcoming events and excursions and make bookings for you if required. They also have a bureau de change (no commission but a slightly lower rate). The two tourist information offices at Centraal Station are always very busy (open daily 8am-8pm). The one in Leidesplein (open daily 8am-7pm) is far less crowded, but it's best to find out as much information as possible prior to your trip.

Museum hours

Most museums are open from 10am to 5pm on weekdays and from 1pm on Sundays. Some close on Mondays. The large museums (Rijksmuseum, Van Gogh and Stedelijk) are open every day from 10am to 5pm. On national holidays, they follow the Sunday opening times, except for 1 January, 25 December and 30 April, when they're closed all day. On presentation of a valid ID card there are reduced rates for students and senior citizens (over 65), as well as reductions for under 18s. 'Museum Cards' are available in VVV and NBT offices and participating museums – valid for a year, they give free admission to all the main museums, but for a price.

Useful addresses

Centrale Medical Service
☎ 592 34 34
Police
Main station, Elandsgracht, 117
☎ 559 91 11;
Lijnbaansgracht, 219;
Nieuwezijds Voorburgwal, 104;
Prinsengracht, 1109.
Emergencies ☎ 112
Lost property
Schiphol airport ☎ 649 14 33;
Trains (5am-midnight)
☎ 557 85 44;
Trams, bus, metro ☎ 460 58 58.
If you lose anything in the street, contact the local police station first, then the police lost property service ☎ 559 30 05

Canals: a user's guide

In Amsterdam the main canals (Prinsengracht, Keizersgracht, Herengracht and Singelgracht) are numbered from 1 to 600 at least. So before setting off, check which side you're on and the direction in which you are heading.

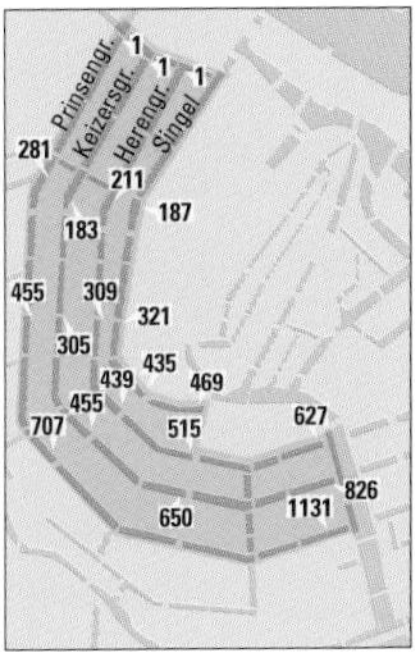

The Béguinage:
a real sense of the past

A stone's throw from the bustle of Kalverstraat, the Béguinage is an island of calm on Spui square, an elegant, triangular space where history and culture meet. You'll also find the city's most famous 'brown café' here, as well as two trendy cafés which face each other, and a great bookshop. The Béguinage is thought to have taken its name from a Flemish preacher, Lambert Le Bègue, who was influential in Flanders.

❶ Spui ★

Once home to the *Provos,* who used to dance madly round the statue of 't Lievertje, a kind of Amsterdam street urchin symbolising their rebellious spirit. The square has since been restored and is now the cultural heart of Amsterdam. A market for old books is held there every Friday and one for contemporary art every Sunday.

❷ The Béguinage ★★★ *(Begijnhof)*

Entrance on Spui indicated by a carved sign.
Open every day 10am-5pm.
Free entry.

A narrow, vaulted passageway leads to this charming garden surrounded by 17th and 18th-century houses. The devout, celibate Béguine nuns have been replaced by old ladies or women students of slender means. In the centre of the lawn stands a medieval church, while number 34 is the city's oldest house, built of wood and dating from 1477.

❸ Gallery of the Civil Guard★ *(Schuttersgalerij)*

Open Mon.-Fri. 10am-5pm, Sat. and Sun. 11am-5pm.
Free entry.

This covered passage, between the historical museum and the Béguine convent, houses huge portraits of the civil guard who were charged with

protecting one of the eleven districts of the city. These men, dressed as archers, crossbow-men and soldiers, look as if they spent more time dining than on the battlefield!

4 Amsterdam Historical Museum ★★ *(Amsterdams Historisch Museum)*

Kalverstraat, 92
Nieuwezijds Voorburgwal, 357
☎ 523 18 22
Open Mon.-Fri. 10am-5pm, Sat. and Sun. 11am-5pm. Entry charge.

History unfolds step by step in this very informative museum housed in a former orphanage for boys and girls, built in the 15th century and extended in the 17th. Everyday life in Amsterdam since the 13th century is evoked through art, maps and models.

5 Café Hoppe★★

Spui, 18-20
☎ 420 44 20.
Open every day 8am-1am

A real Amsterdam institution, Café Hoppe has been popular with both locals and passers-by since 1670. The narrow, wood-panelled, smoke-filled room, with its sawdust-covered floor, is always full to bursting point, but definitely worth a visit!

6 Lucius★★

(fish restaurant)
Spuistraat, 247
☎ 624 18 31
Open every day except Sun. 5pm-midnight.

This is the best fish restaurant in town. Simply decorated with pottery and rustic tables, the dishes of the day are chalked up on a blackboard. Here you can eat fish and seafood specialities, served without fuss, and with a great choice of liqueurs and spirits to round off your meal.

7 Vrankrijk Squat ★

Spuistraat, 199-216.

Although squatting may have gone out of style, a few of the indomitable old guard bought their squat and turned the former home of the *Handelsblad* daily newspaper into a kind of monument to the huge 'Provo' protest movement, which flourished in the 1970s. Today the grunge evenings, highly-coloured graffiti and 'kill the pigs' sign on the façade of the building are just a pale reflection of the way things used to be.

8 Atheneum Boekhandel★

Spui, 14-16
☎ 622 62 48
Open Mon. 11am-6pm, Tue.-Sat. 9.30am-6pm, Sun. noon-5.30pm, Thu. until 9pm.

Like the square, this lovely bookshop, with its Art Nouveau-style decor, is very elegant and extremely busy. Try the main shop for the latest best-seller or a selection of CDs. If you're looking for a foreign language newspaper, go to the annexe next door.

The Dam,
heart of the city

This is the beating heart of the city, where there's always something going on amid the neon signs and fast-food outlets. Around the square, fine monuments testify to the Calvinist philosophy of money, religion and hard work, values attacked by the *Provos,* who made their headquarters here. The city's ugliest monument, a concrete obelisk commemorating Dutch victims of war, has become a meeting point for new-style hippies, punks and a variety of lost souls.

❶ Royal Palace★ *(Koninklijk Paleis)*

☎ 624 86 98
Open every day Jun.-Jul. 10am-6pm, Aug. noon-5.30pm, Sep.-May 1-4pm; opening hours may vary during official functions. Entry charge.

Before becoming Louis Bonaparte's royal residence, this inelegant, austere building was the town hall, designed by the famous 17th-century architect Jacob van Campen. Don't miss the superb tiled floor in the Burghers' Hall *(Burgerzaal)* decorated with maps of the northern and southern hemispheres. Today the queen comes here only for official receptions.

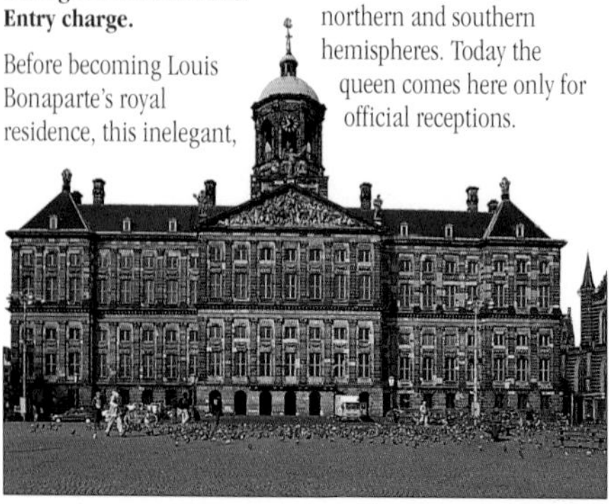

❷ New Church★★ *(Nieuwe Kerk)*

Dam
☎ 638 69 09
Open every day 10am-6pm during temporary exhibitions. Entry charge.

This church was built in the flamboyant Gothic style and has been modified many times over the years. Today it houses exhibitions and concerts. Its stained glass, bronze chandeliers, mahogany pulpit (1649) and superb choir stalls are perfectly complemented by the sparse, Calvinist interior.

All the kings and queens of the Netherlands have been crowned here in accordance with tradition.

❸ Palette★

Nieuwezijds Voorburgwal, 125
☎ 639 32 07
Open Sat. 11am-5pm and by appointment weekdays.

Leaning up against the New Church is the city's smallest shop, specialising in making silk and satin shoes. With a choice of over 500 colours, there's no way you could fail to find just the right shoes and accessories to go with your favourite evening dress.

❹ Hotel Krasnapolsky★

Dam, 9
☎ 554 91 11
Open 24 hours every day.

Make sure you have your lunch, or even just a cup of tea, in this 19th-century palace. An immense, amazing winter garden which recalls the magnificence of the Belle Époque. The decor in the restaurant consists of black and white floor tiles, frescoes on the walls and large palms, and, to cap it all, the food is excellent too (buffet lunch and breakfast).

❺ Beurs van Berlage ★★★

Damrak, 277
☎ 530 41 13
Museum open Tue.-Sun. 10am-4pm.

This imposing building sited along Damrak, has a red-brick façade 141m/463ft-long designed by H.P. Berlage. In 1903 its sober, functional style represented a complete

break with the past. There's a fine view of the city from the top of its 39m/128ft tower if you can manage the 95 very steep steps. The large hall with its perfect acoustics, home of the Netherlands Philharmonic Orchestra, stages concerts all year round.

❻ De Drie Fleschjes★★

Gravenstraat, 18
☎ 624 84 43
Open Mon.-Sat. noon-8.30pm, Sun. 3-7pm.

The city's finest *proeflokaal* was first founded by the Bootz distillery in 1650. This is the place where journalists and stockbrokers congregate at the end of the day, hanging their jackets on the taps of the barrels before drinking a few *borrels* of *jenever*. They also have a unique collection of portraits of the mayors of Amsterdam here, all painted on little bottles.

❼ Magna Plazza★

Nieuwezijds Voorburgwal, 182
☎ 626 91 99
Open Mon. 11am-7pm, Tue.-Wed., Fri.-Sat. 10am-7pm, Sun. noon-7pm, Thu. 10am-9pm.

Cornelis Peters, architect of this pretentious neo-Gothic construction in brick and white stone, received more than a few sarcastic comments back in 1899. Originally the central post office, it has since been transformed into an elegant shopping centre. The stairwell is worth seeing.

Rokin: for a saturday afternoon stroll

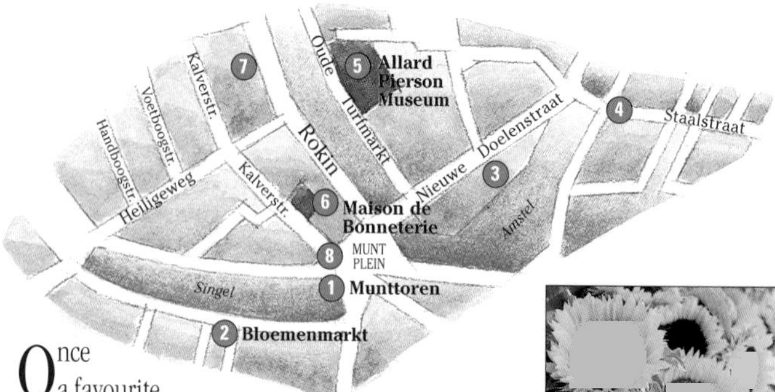

Once a favourite haunt of Amsterdam's bourgeoisie, who would promenade along the side of the inner dock *(rak-in)*, this was home to the most prestigious establishments in the city. The large banks, the best diamond merchants, the most prominent antique dealers and *Hajenius*, cigar-makers since 1826, all could boast that their clientele included royalty. Today the dock has been filled in to make way for cars and trams, and the prestige businesses find themselves sharing their space with other, less exclusive shops.

❶ Mint Tower★ *(Munttoren)*

Muntplein, 12.

In 1620 Hendrick de Keyser, the foremost architect of the

time, used the remains of an old city gate as a base on which to build a Baroque wooden bell tower. Nowadays the chimes ring out every quarter of an hour. The tiny shop on the ground floor sells authentic Delft and Makkum ware, both modern and period, and is well worth a visit.

❷ Flower Market ★★ *(Bloemenmarkt)*

Singel
Open Mon.-Sat. 8am-5.30pm, also Sun. 9am-5pm in summer.

The flower-sellers' barges are permanently moored to the

banks of the Singel, forming a brightly-coloured floating market. It's always a pleasure to wander past the stalls covered in bouquets of cut and dried flowers, displaying valuable bonsai trees, or simply piled high with a variety of bulbs.

❸ Café De Jaren★

Nieuwe Doelenstraat, 20-22
☎ 625 57 71
Open every day 10am-1am (2am Fri-Sat).

This is the trendiest of the large cafés, located along the Amstel and designed by Onno de Vries. It's wonderfully light and spacious, and in fine weather it's hard to find a free table on the wide floating terrace. A favourite haunt of students and businessmen alike, who come here for a late breakfast or quick lunch.

❹ Staalstraat★★

This charming street straddles two canals by means of drawbridges. It's home to a number of shops, including the art bookshop *Nijhot & Lee* and *Puccini* the confectioner's. The lovely gabled house at number 7b is the former drapers' hall, headquarters of the drapers' guild whose portraits were painted by Rembrandt (*Drapers Syndic,* Rijksmuseum, see p. 62).

❺ Allard Pierson Museum★★

Oude Turfmarkt, 127
☎ 525 25 56
Open Tue.-Fri. 10am-5pm, Sat., Sun. and bank holidays 1-5pm. Entry charge.

This pint-sized and highly educational archeological museum is perfect for learning about the daily life of the Mediterranean peoples of antiquity by means of objects and models. You can write your name in hieroglyphs on a computer or admire beautiful Parthian and Sassanid jewellery.

❻ Maison de Bonneterie★

Rokin, 140
☎ 531 34 00
Open Mon.1-5.30pm, Tue.-Sat. 10am-5.30pm late opening Thu., Sun. noon-5pm.

This is a real old-fashioned department store, boasting the title 'Supplier to the Queen'. It has three floors where you can still buy timeless, quality products such as classic, hard-wearing English clothing for the whole family, or a set of golf clubs and accessories. The brasserie on the first floor is just as quaint, filled with respectable old ladies taking their afternoon tea.

❼ P.G.C. Hajenius★★

Rokin, 92-96
☎ 623 74 94
Open Mon. noon-6pm, Tue.-Sat. 9.30am-6pm, Thu. until 9pm, Sun. noon-6pm.

This place really is an Amsterdam institution. The prestigious

❽ Andries de Jong Ship Shop★

Muntplein, 8
☎ 624 52 51
Open Mon.-Fri. 9am-5.30pm, Sat. 9.30am-5.30pm.

If you've always dreamed of turning your home into a pleasure-cruiser, look no further. This shop sells barometers, storm-lamps, cabin lamps, pirate flags, compasses and every other conceivable gadget for people with a passion for ships and sailing.

Hajenius cigar-maker's, with its cosy decor of cedarwood, marble, lamps and accessories in pure Art Deco style, has been making subtly-blended, aromatic cigars for 175 years.

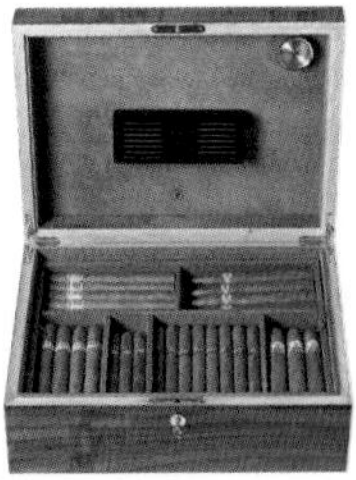

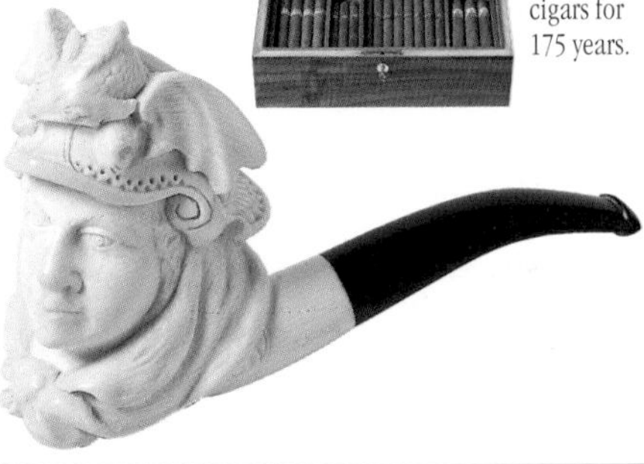

From Nieuwmarkt to Prinsenhof: the real Amsterdam

The shady canals are lined with traditional shops and former convents, now converted into cafés, giving this picturesque university quarter its special character. Here you'll find experimental theatres and secondhand book stalls, cannabis-smokers and herring-eaters. This is village Amsterdam, where everybody knows everybody else.

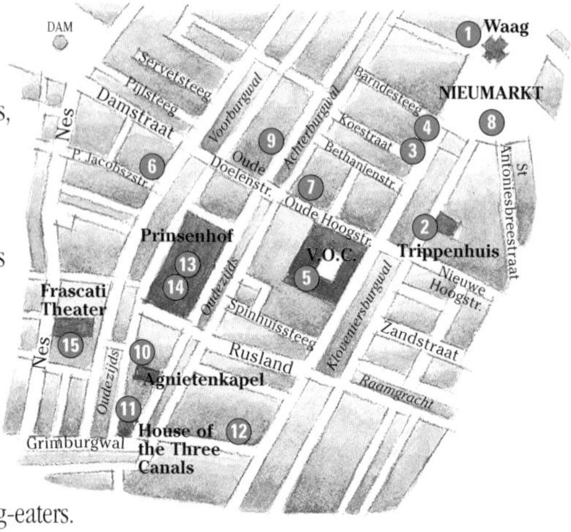

❶ Waag★
Nieuwmarkt, 4
☎ 422 77 72.

In the 17th century the massive tower of the St Anthony Gate, a rare remnant of the medieval fortified wall, was once used as the public weighing station *(waag)*. The hall on the upper floor was later occupied by the Surgeons' Guild, the central tower housing an anatomical theatre where Rembrandt painted his famous picture *The Anatomy Lesson of Professor Tulp*. Decorated by Dijkmann, today the hall is home to a friendly Internet café and restaurant, lit entirely by candles, which gives it quite a magical ambience when night falls. Every day, from 10am to midnight, you can eat organic food, get online or simply have a coffee and read the paper in the most favourable vantage point to enjoy the Nieuwmarkt scene.

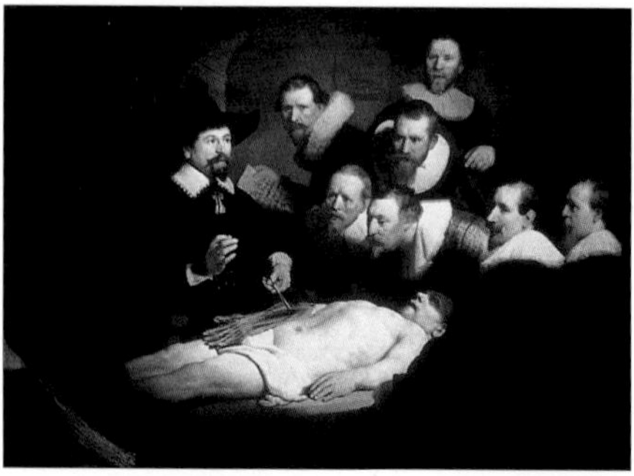

❷ Trippenhuis★★
Kloveniersburgwal, 29.

This imposing old building, built in the Renaissance style in 1660, is one of the few in Amsterdam that can compete with the grandeur of Venetian palaces. Its owners, the Trip brothers, made their fortunes from the arms trade. Across the canal at no. 26, you can see the much smaller house which was once the home of their coachman.

❸ Jacob Hooy & Co. Herbalists★

Kloveniersburgwal, 12
☎ 624 30 41
Open Mon. 10am-6pm, Tue.-Fri. 8.15am-6pm, Sat. 8.15am-5pm.

For a hundred and fifty years members of the Oldeboom family have stood behind the counter of this deliciously spicy-smelling shop. The wooden casks that line the shelves and the polished drawers contain around six hundred different aromatic plants. The delicious liquorice sweets are not to be missed.

❹ Café Maximiliaan★★

Kloveniersburgwal, 6-8
☎ 626 62 80
Open every day except Mon. from 3pm.

This café-brasserie is located on the site of the former Bethany convent. It specialises in strong, amber-coloured beers, which are brewed in huge copper vats in a room at the back. They also sell wonderful food here, made from recipes that include beer in the ingredients.

❺ The V.O.C. building

Oude Hoogstraat, 24.

In the 17th and 18th centuries this large building of red brick and yellow stone, bearing the monogram of the *Vereenige Oostindische Compagnie*, was the headquarters of the very

famous Dutch East India Company, which imported spices, coloured fabrics and porcelain from the East. Public sales of these goods were held twice yearly in the courtyard.

❻ Manus Magnus★★

Oudezijds Voorburgwal, 258
☎ 622 68 12
Open Mon. 1-5pm, Tue. and Thu. 10am-3pm, Wed. and Fri. 3pm-6pm, weekends by appointment.

Manus Magnus works with gold and silver to create stunning items such as dishes and candlesticks, with mirror-smooth or brushed surfaces across which the light dances. When he mixes the two metals his creations have an organic feel, shining like drops of sunshine. If you have a particular idea in mind, you can commission him to realise the design for you.

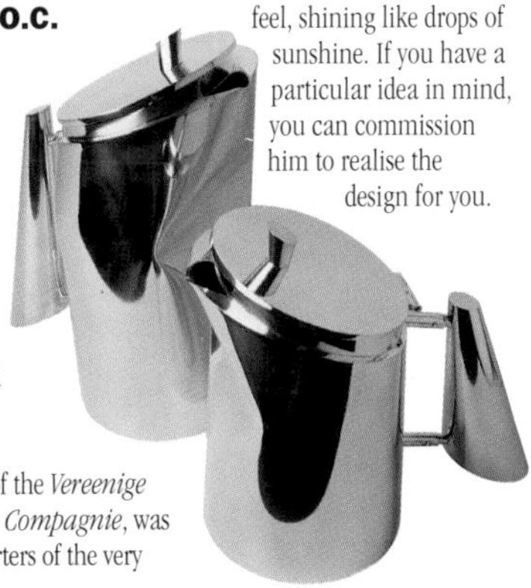

7 Capsicum★★

Oude Hoogstraat, 1
☎ 623 10 16
Open Mon. 1-6pm, Tue.-Sat. 10am-6pm, Thu. until 9pm.

The sparkling colours in this classy shop rival any Eastern bazaar. Here you can buy your upholstery and dress-making fabrics accompanied by the sound of soothing classical music. You'll find linens, cottons and silks, mostly from India and Thailand, including a wonderful range

of embroidered silks (their speciality) and batik fabrics, as well as the more everyday muslin and cotton tie-dye materials. Expect to pay between €20 and €59 per metre for plain fabric.

8 Nieuwmarkt Square

The city council called on two Dutch sculptors, Alexander Schabracq and Tom Postma, to revamp Nieuwmarkt. These two artisans, who also worked on Damrak, are responsible for the lamp posts and green railings inspired by Russian Constructivism. Not everybody likes these new additions, but at least they don't get in anyone's way.

9 Museum of Marijuana★

Oudezijds Achterburgwal, 148
☎ 623 59 61
Open every day 11am-10pm
Entry charge.

If you want to know more about marijuana and its various uses, come to this museum, the only one of its kind in Europe. It retraces ten thousand years of the history of the cannabis plant and you'll discover how, before being grown illicitly in people's cellars and sold in smokable form in coffee-shops, it was used extensively in the port of Amsterdam… but only in the manufacture of hemp ropes.

10 Chapel of St Agnes★ *(Agnietenkapel)*

Oudezijds Voorburgwal, 231
☎ 525 33 39
University museum open Mon.-Fri. 9am-5pm
Entry charge.

Apart from the chapel, built in 1397, all the buildings belonging to the former medieval convent of the Agnites were given the new name of *Illustrae Atheneum*,

the city's first university, in 1632. On the first floor you can see the oldest teaching room in Amsterdam, a lecture theatre with a beautiful painted ceiling decorated with Renaissance motifs, which is still in use today.

11 House of the Three Canals★★

Intersection of Oudezijds Voorburgwal, Oudezijds Achterburgwal and Grimburgwal canals.

This fine old building from the golden age of the 17th-century, with its distinctive red shutters

and two-tone façade, was built at the point where three canals meet and was the last building to the south-east of the medieval city. Today it's home to a publishing house.

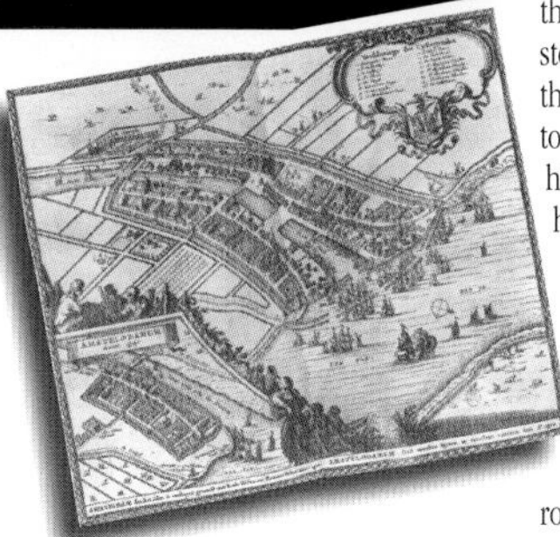

⓬ Oude Manhuispoort Passage★

Book fair
Every day 10am-6pm.

The secondhand booksellers set up their stalls in the niches of the covered passageway that links two canals, the Oudezijds Achterburgwal and the Kloveniersburgwal.

When you've had a good rummage, take a look at the lovely inner courtyard of the University of Amsterdam and sort through some of the old engravings which will transport you back to an Amsterdam of years gone by.

⓭ Prinsenhof★★★ (The Grand Hotel)

Oudezijds Voorburgwal, 197
☎ 555 35 60.

In the 16th century this luxury hotel was the residence of princes. It's still called the 'Court of Princes' despite the fact that it was the town hall until 1986, after the town hall on the Dam was transformed into the royal palace. In 1966, the marriage of Queen Beatrix was celebrated in the Art Deco wedding hall.

⓮ Café Roux★

Oudezijds Voorburgwal, 197
☎ 555 35 60
Open every day.

This Art Deco brasserie is one of the best addresses in Amsterdam if you like French regional cooking, or just fancy a good cup of tea. An emotive fresco painted by Karel Appel in 1949 adorns the walls. Travelling by train across war-torn Europe, the sight of wide-eyed children, holding out their hands for food at every stop, became firmly fixed in the artist's mind, and he chose to depict this subject here – his way of paying the taxes he owed to the Town Hall.

⓯ Frascati Theater★

Nes, 63
☎ 626 68 66.

In this long, narrow road you'll find a small experimental theatre specialising in plays and choreography of a resolutely contemporary kind. You don't always have to understand Dutch to watch one of these sometimes unnerving shows. The café next door, which serves light meals until midnight, is frequented mainly by theatrical types.

The red light district: where anything goes

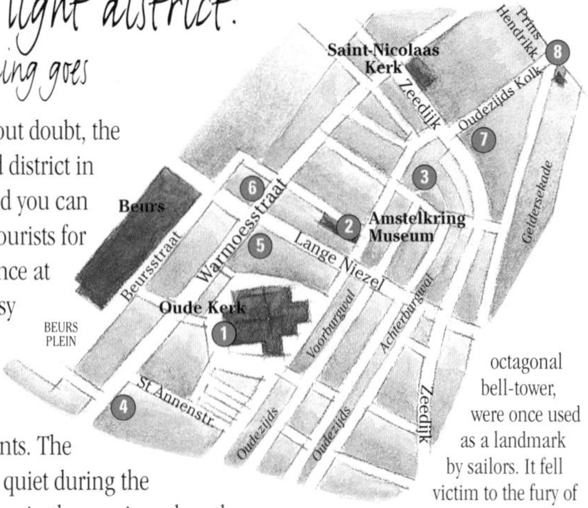

This is, without doubt, the most visited district in Amsterdam, and you can hardly blame tourists for sneaking a glance at the ladies of easy virtue who are displayed in the windows, waiting for clients. The district is fairly quiet during the day, but livens up in the evening when the neon signs light up. The curious public crowd the quaysides, accosted by pimps and dealers and beguiled by the oriental scents wafting from *Zeedijk* and the discreet Chinatown of Amsterdam. The biggest irony is that this somewhat unholy district also has three churches, one of which is hidden away in an attic.

❶ Old Church★★ *(Oude Kerk)*

Oude Kerksplein, 23
☎ 625 82 84
Open Sun. 4-5pm, bell-ringing concert.

This church, the oldest building in the city, seems like an ancient ship, abandoned in an ocean of sin. Its buildings, especially the Gothico-Renaissance-style octagonal bell-tower, were once used as a landmark by sailors. It fell victim to the fury of the Calvinists in the late 16th century and was stripped of its sculptures, which explains the sparseness of its interior. It is now occasionally used for concerts and exhibitions.

❷ Amstelkring Museum★★★

Oudezijds Voorburgwal, 40
☎ 624 66 04
Open Mon.-Sat. 10am-5pm, Sun. 1-5pm
Entry charge.

The attic of this pretty bourgeois house conceals a clandestine Catholic chapel, which was set up in 1663 after Catholics lost their right to public worship. The house itself is also worth a visit for its heavy Dutch furniture, its tablecloths, its two kitchens with their Delft tiles and its many nooks and crannies.

❸ Oudezijds Voorburgwal★

It was probably inevitable that this canal, a stone's throw from the old port, would become the headquarters of the city's red light district. In red neon-lit windows, scantily-clad women make phone calls, dance, read magazines or simply watch the passers-by to pass the time between clients. Here there's no mistaking what trade is being plied.

4 Condomerie Het Gulden Vlies

Warmoesstraat, 141
☎ 627 41 74
Open Mon.-Sat. 11am-6pm.

The threat of AIDS has boosted the sale of condoms, which now come in an amazing range of colours and tastes, and some very improbable shapes, such as cow's udders, hands, Mickey mouse figures and dummies. Plenty of amusing gift ideas.

5 Geels & Co★★

Warmoesstraat, 67
☎ 624 06 83
Open Mon.-Sat. 9.30am-6pm.

This shop has been selling excellent coffee, ground on the premises, for the last hundred

and fifty years. The owners will be only too pleased to show you their collection of grinding machines and mills on display upstairs.

6 Het Karbeel

Warmoesstraat, 58
☎ 627 49 95
Open every day 10am-midnight.

No one would guess the secret that lies beneath this quiet little café-restaurant. Used as an inn since the 16th century, a large underground tunnel (still in existence) was dug in the 17th century, all the way to Damrak, so that smugglers could move their contraband in and out of the city.

7 Cirelli restaurant★★

Oudezijdskolk, 69
☎ 624 35 12
Open every day after 6pm, closed Sun. in winter. Booking advisable.

This former warehouse, renovated with a touch of imagination, serves the best pasta in town. Make sure you see the central table sculpture by Alexander Schabracq and the wonderful lamps.

8 The Tower of Weeping Women★ *(Schreierstoren)*

Prins Hendrikkade, 94-95
☎ 624 80 52
Bar open Mon. 10am-9pm, Tue.-Thu. 10am-1am, Sat. 10am-3am, Sun. 11am-8pm.

It's said that from this tower sailors' wives would watch their menfolk sail away, possibly never to return. It now houses

a shop selling almanacs, sky charts and the very valuable *Bolle* barometers, as well as a bar, the *V.O.C. Café* on the first floor, with regular live music and a good range of liqueurs and *jenevers*.

Saint-Nicolaas Kerk

In the late 16th century Catholics lost their Saint-Nicolaas Kerk, the present-day Oude Kerk, and were forced to gather in secret chapels. It was not until the 19th century that Catholics finally regained their church, and the new Saint-Nicolaas Kerk on Prins Hendrikkade was consecrated on the 7 February 1887. One of the better known new churches, it's tall and spacious with a beautiful, well-kept interior.

The old Jewish quarter: a thriving district

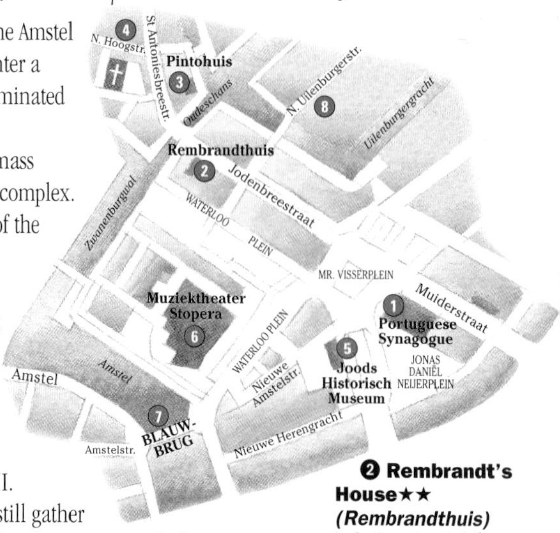

Cross over the Amstel and you enter a ghost town dominated by the highly controversial mass of the Stopera complex. The building of the metro and the drive towards better housing have all but finished the destruction that began in World War II. Jewish people still gather here on Saturdays for services in the large synagogue but, apart from that, the flea market on Waterlooplein is the only thing that brings a little life to the district.

1 Portuguese Synagogue★★★ (*Esnoga*)

Mr Visserplein, 3
☎ 624 53 51
Open Sun.-Fri. 10am-4pm. Entry charge.

This enormous brick cube with its huge windows is actually a synagogue, and one of the most beautiful in Europe. Financed by the community of 'Portuguese' Jews, descended from those driven out of Portugal by the Spanish Inquisition, it miraculously still looks just the way it did when it was first opened back in 1675.

2 Rembrandt's House★★ (*Rembrandthuis*)

Jodenbreestraat, 4-6
☎ 520 04 00
Open Mon.-Sat. 10am-5pm, Sun. 1-5pm. Entry charge.

Rembrandt bought this superb Renaissance house in 1639 with his wife Saskia's dowry. He lived here for 20 years, painting his finest pictures in his first-floor studio. But a different aspect of the artist's formidable talent is on show here in a display of 250 engravings arranged by theme, including genre scenes, self portraits, nudes and landscapes.

3 Pintohuis★
Sint Antoniebreestraat, 69
☎ 624 31 84
Open by appointment.

In 1651 Isaac Pinto, a rich Jewish banker, spent the tidy sum of 35,000 florins building himself this lovely Italianate palace, which certainly comes as a surprise in this much

altered district. Indeed it once almost disappeared as a result of a road-building project.

4 Joe's Vliegerwinkel★
Nieuwe Hoogstraat, 19
☎ 625 01 39
Open Mon. 1pm-6pm, Tue.-Fri. 11am-6pm, Sat. 11am-5pm.

A real delight for children of all ages, this shop, packed full of kites in all shapes and sizes, is definitely worth a detour. Made on the premises or imported from China and the USA, the kites are made from multicoloured nylon, and have all been selected for their sheer beauty and originality.

5 Museum of Jewish History★ *(Joods Historisch Museum)*
Jonas Daniel Meijerplein, 2-4
☎ 626 99 45
Open every day 11am-5pm
Entry charge.

This museum is housed in four synagogues of the Ashkenazi community, linked by glass-covered walkways. Objects, photos and documents are arranged by theme to illustrate the life and culture of the Jews who have lived in Amsterdam since the late 16th century.

6 Muziektheater 'Stopera'★★
Waterlooplein, 22,
☎ 551 89 11
Amstel, 3
☎ 551 91 11.

The enormous complex that dominates the Amstel houses the new town hall and a concert hall with seats for 1,600 people. The building's highly controversial aesthetics and the extra destruction it necessitated in a district that had already been blighted by town planners, generated some violent reactions. It opened in 1986 and is still known as the 'Stopera', the name given to it by its critics. It does, however, have remarkable acoustics and is home to the Netherlands Opera and the Dutch National Ballet.

7 Blue Bridge★ *(Blauwbrug)*
Built for the universal exhibition of 1883, this bridge crosses the majestic Amstel. It was this river which gave rise to the city itself, as well as its name of 'Amstel-dam'.

8 Gassan Diamonds★★★
Nieuwe Uilen Burgerstraat, 173-175
☎ 622 53 33
Open every day 9am-5pm, with free tours every 20 minutes
Free entry.

Gassan is the biggest diamond house in Holland. An expert guide will show you the cutters and polishers at work, and explain all about facets, what makes a diamond valuable and, above all, the traps to avoid when making a purchase. The best time to take a tour is first thing in the morning or between 1pm and 3pm, when it's quieter.

Jordaan, from cafés to culture

This is the district that Amsterdammers like best. With its tight network of narrow streets and houses, its nicotine-stained 'brown cafés', little courtyards full of flowers, tiny shops, barge-filled canals and colourful bird market, it's here that the very soul of Amsterdam lies. The district was built outside the city walls in the 17th century, to house working class labourers and craftsmen, with Prinsengracht forming a natural border with the world of the wily bourgeoisie. Although somewhat gentrified these days, it retains its own language and folklore, which come intensely alive during the Jordaan festival in September.

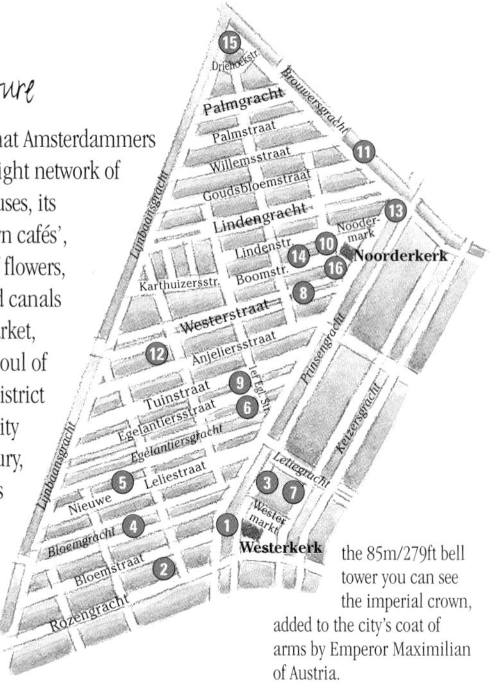

❶ Western Church★★ *(Westerkerk)*

Westerplein
Bell tower open Apr.-Sep. Mon.-Sat. 10am-4pm, bell-ringing concert noon-1pm
Entry charge.

Regarded as Hendrick de Keyser's masterpiece, this was the first Renaissance-style church to be built after the Reformation. At the top of the 85m/279ft bell tower you can see the imperial crown, added to the city's coat of arms by Emperor Maximilian of Austria.

❷ Coppenhagen, 1001 Kralen★

Rozengracht, 54
☎ 624 36 81
Open Mon. 1-6pm, Tue.-Fri. 10am-6pm, Sat. 10am-5pm.

On the shelves of this shop you'll see hundreds of jars filled with gleaming glass beads of every conceivable colour, including antique beads from Murano and Bohemia, which were once used to trade with African princes, and more recently-made beads from India, Indonesia, Germany and Venice.

❸ Anne Frank's House★

Prinsengracht, 263
☎ 556 71 00
Open every day 9am-5pm and Apr.-Aug. 9am-9pm
Entry charge.

If you're not put off by the long queues, you can visit the *achterhuis*, or 'house behind',

where the teenage Anne Frank lived hidden away with the rest of her family, eight people in all, for two years before being deported and dying in Belsen concentration camp. Her personal diary, which gives a poignant account of this time, has been published in almost fifty different languages. The money raised from sales of the book is partly used to fund the Anne Frank Foundation, which combats racism.

❹ Bloemgracht★

In the 17th century the 'canal of flowers' was inhabited by cloth-dyers. Today it's one of

the smartest canals in Jordaan, lined with beautiful gabled houses bearing coats of arms identifying the trades of the occupants. Three of these, numbers 87, 89 and 91 have attractive façades, typical of canal houses.

❺ Sint Andrieshofje★★

Egelantiersgracht, 107
Free entry.

Step through the door beneath the coat of arms and, at the end of a

corridor with a Delft tiled floor, you'll be surprised to find a very small garden full of flowers *(hof)* surrounded by tiny houses, once occupied by elderly people in need. This former Beguine convent, founded in 1616, is today one of the most sought-after places in the city and a house here is cripplingly expensive.

❻ 't Smalle★★

Egelantiersgracht, 12
☎ 623 96 17
Open Mon.-Fri. 10am-1am, Sat. and Sun. 10am-2am.

This café has been a popular venue in the Jordaan district since 1780, so the nicotine has had more than enough time to impregnate its walls and furniture. Note the pretty enamelled stained-glass windows and polished tables and chairs. Queen Beatrix herself came here to sample the cosy atmosphere, but she stayed outside on the floating terrace, which is set out at the first hint of sunny weather.

❼ Greenpeace★
Corner of Keizersgracht and Leliegracht.

The ecological organisation Greenpeace is housed in this very fine Art Nouveau building designed by Gerrit van Arkel and dating from 1905. The imposing façade is enlivened with mosaics, bow windows and pinnacles. Have a look at the entrance hall as well, which is decorated with ceramics.

❽ Mecanisch Speelgoed★
Westerstraat, 67
☎ 638 16 80
Open every day except Wed. 10am-6pm.

This little shop sells reproductions of lovely old-fashioned toys, the sort that your grandparents used to play with. The two floors are piled high with masks, games that require patience and skill, and a variety of painted metal clockwork toys.

❾ Claes Claesz in de Jordaan
Egelantiersstraat, 24-26
☎ 625 53 06
Open every day exc. Mon. 10am-11pm.

Step through the wooden door and you'll find yourself in one of Jordaan's secret places, a former hospice founded by a rich draper in 1616. Today's lucky residents are all students at the conservatory of music, which has taken the place over. The little adjoining restaurant serves generous portions of unpretentious food, to the accompaniment of singing at weekends.

❿ Noordermarkt★
On Monday mornings there's a bric-a-brac market here, and on Saturday mornings a very picturesque market with homing pigeons, exotic birds and cages full of cheeping chicks ranged alongside the stalls selling fresh farm produce.

⓫ Brouwersgracht ★★
The Brewers' Canal marks the northernmost edge of this district. With its many bridges, red-shuttered warehouses converted into lofts and flower-covered houseboats

15 VAN WEES *JENEVER*★

Driehoeckstraat, at the very end of Brouwersgracht, is home to the oldest distillery in the Netherlands, owned by the Van Wees family, who have passed down the secret of making a *jenever* flavoured with herbs from generation to generation. If you want to sample the product, however, you have to keep going a little further, to 'De Admiral' *proeflokaal* at Herengracht, 319.

moored along the quaysides, this is one of the most picturesque views in the city.

12 Horeca Antiek Garage★

Westerstraat, 10-12
☎ 423 32 16
Open Mon. 9am-5pm, Tue.-Fri. 11am-5.30pm, Sat. 11am-5pm.

Someone with a good sense of humour was behind this café-cum-bric-a-brac store. Sit down and enjoy a coffee and *speculaas* at one end or, at the other, rummage through the old furniture (mostly from bars) and a whole jumble of other odd curiosities.

't Papeneiland★★

Prinsengracht, 2
☎ 624 19 89
Open Mon.-Thu. 10am-1am, Fri., Sat. 10am-3am, Sun. noon-1am.

Gleaming beer pumps, an old cast iron stove in the middle of the room and walls lined with Delft

tiles make up the decor of this little 'brown café', which has been popular with the locals since 1642.

14 Koevoet★

Lindenstraat, 17
☎ 624 08 46
Dinner after 6pm, except Mon.

An unpretentious little *eetcafé* of the kind that flourishes so busily all over Jordaan. You enter via an old bar with a well-worn floor, then climbing some steps, you reach the small dining room itself, where you'll find a few buffet tables set out in a welcoming manner.

16 Northern Church *(Noorderkerk)*

This is the Western Church's smaller sister-church, and was designed by the same architect. It was specially built for the Protestant inhabitants of Jordaan, who found the Westerkerk too grand for their comfort. This is one of the few churches where services are still held.

Rembrandtplein: art by day, clubs by night

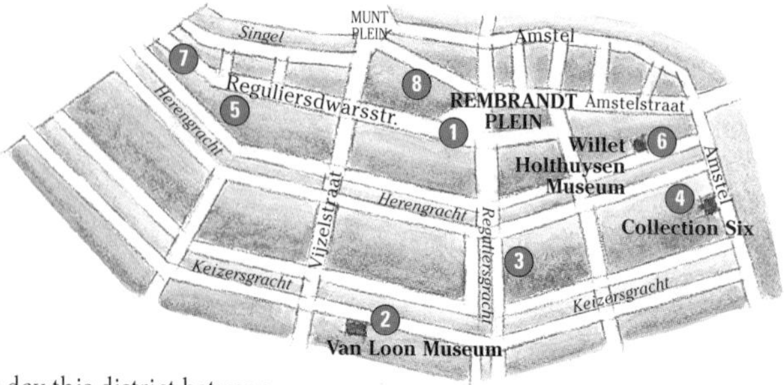

By day this district between the Amstel and Keizersgracht is a place of quiet squares and shady canals whose still waters mirror the magnificent façades of palacial residences, some of which deign to open their doors and reveal their secrets to passers-by. But once the strings of lights between the seven bridges of Reguliersgracht are switched on, the night revellers invade the streets and the area reveals its livelier side, full of fast food outlets and gay bars.

❶ Rembrandtplein ★

Former home to the old butter market, the square was renamed after the great 17th-century master painter, whose statue stands in its centre. Today it's full of cafés, of varying degrees of stylishness, with tables and chairs spilling out over the pavement, and is one of the main hangouts for young Amsterdammers.

❷ Van Loon Museum★★★

Keizersgracht, 672
☎ 624 52 55
Open Fri.-Mon. 11am-5pm.
Entry charge.

The heir to the Van Loon fortune has opened the doors of his family residence, inviting you into the cosseted world of the 18th-century patrician. With its silk-lined rooms, chests made from exotic wood, family portraits and tables displaying valuable porcelain, this is one of the city's most delightful places.

3 Hooghoudt★★
Reguliersgracht, 11
☎ 420 40 41
Open every day 4pm-1am.

Once the working day is over, this *proeflokaal,* housed in an old 17th-century warehouse, fills up and doesn't empty until closing-time. Here they drink Groningen *jenever*, which is kept in earthenware jars to preserve its special flavour. Start by ordering an iced *korenwijn* (wheat wine).

4 Collection Six★★
Amstel, 218
☎ 622 44 10
Private collection.
Visit by appointment only, with tickets bought from the Rijksmuseum.

Admirably located on the Amstel, this elegant house is still inhabited by the descendants of the 'Six', who were Huguenot refugees from Saint-Omer in France. Famous as art-lovers, they acquired one of the finest collections of 17th-century paintings, including exceptional works by Rembrandt and Frans Hals.

5 Het Tuynhuys★
Reguliersdwarsstraat, 28
☎ 627 66 03
Open Mon.-Fri. noon-2.30pm, every day 6.30-10.30pm.

This former carriage-shed, hidden behind the flower market, was designed by the photographer and interior designer Kees Hageman. In summer you can eat in the beautiful garden to the sound of a flute. The tempting set meals and varied à la carte menu change with the seasons.

6 Willet Holthuysen Museum★★
Herengracht, 605
☎ 523 18 70
Open Mon.-Fri. 10am-5pm, Sat. and Sun. 11am-5pm.
Entry charge.

The Willet Holthuysens, the couple who owned this lovely 17th-century residence, were keen collectors of glassware,

7 SATURNIO★
Reguliersdwarsstraat, 5
☎ 639 01 02
Open every day noon-midnight.

A theatrical decor of columns and Moorish mosaics adorns this restaurant, frequented by, among others, the gay community. Sicilian cuisine with delicious escalopes and fish specialities. Dishes of the day are chalked up on the blackboard.

porcelain, silverware and paintings. Experience scenes from the daily life of wealthy 18th-century bourgeois Amsterdammers.

8 Tuschinski Cinema★★
Reguliersbreestraat, 26-28
☎ 626 15 10
Programmes daily.
Guided tours Sun. and Mon. 10am in summer.
Entry charge.

This wonderful 1930s cinema has just undergone a loving programme of restoration. The fabulous Art Deco interior has been returned to its former splendour, and guided tours are available in summer. Films are shown in their original language with Dutch subtitles.

Herengracht, untouched by time

This peaceful canal, lined with magnificent old houses, is the most beautiful in Amsterdam. Its grand residences, whose Baroque pediments and severe façades reflect the character of their wealthy occupants, were designed and decorated by the best artists. To protect the inhabitants' peace, this has always been a strictly residential quarter, and restaurants and cafés have been restricted to the intersecting streets. As a result the district has remained untouched by time and you'll find yourself conjuring up the sound of hooves and carriage wheels on the street or the echoes of grand royal parties.

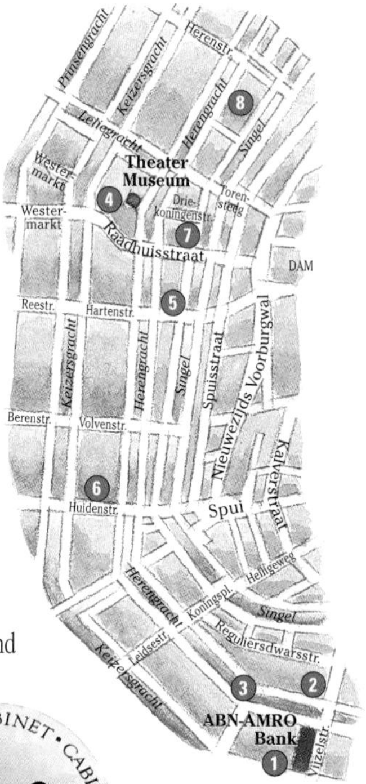

❶ ABN-AMRO Bank★

Vijzelstraat, 66-80.

Yet another illustration of the architectural exuberance that reigned in Amsterdam in the 1920s. This strictly geometrical, multicoloured building, 100m/109 yds long and ten stories high, was designed by K. de Bazel.

❷ Katten Kabinet ★★

Herengracht, 497
☎ 626 53 78
Open 28 Jun.-28 Aug. Tue.- Fri. 10am-2pm, Sat.-Sun. 1-5pm.
Entry charge.

Cats rule in this fine residence from the golden age of the 17th century, with its painted stucco decorations. Not only are they the subject of all the exhibitions held here, but you'll also find live examples curled up in the armchairs or lazing about the garden.

❸ Golden Bend★★ (*Gouden bocht*)

Herengracht, 507, 495, 475, 476 and 478.

At the bend in the canal, you'll find a group of houses that are among the grandest in Amsterdam. Each one occupies a double plot and their proud, austere façades reflect the wealth and self-assurance of the patricians and merchants of the 18th century.

4 Theater Museum ★★

Herengracht, 168
☎ 551 33 00
Open Tue.-Fri. 11am-5pm, Sat. and Sun. 1-5pm.
Entry charge.

Make sure you see the city's finest monumental staircase. It spirals upwards with a false perspective in a hall entirely decorated in stucco and grisaille pictures with mythological themes by Jacob de Wit, an artist much sought after by the wealthy 18th-century bourgeoisie. The museum's other jewel is a miniature theatre (1781) complete with moving sets.

6 Pompadour★

Huidenstraat, 12
☎ 623 95 54
Open Tue.-Fri. 9.30am-6pm, Sat. 9am-5.30pm.

Wealthy Amsterdammers come here to buy Pompadour's own luxury cakes, chocolates and caramels. The adjoining tea-house is always packed out in the afternoon, when the ladies take a break from shopping to refresh their energies.

5 Brilmuseum★

Gasthuismolensteeg, 7
☎ 421 24 14
Open Wed.-Fri. noon-5.30pm, Sat. noon-5pm.

Reconstructed in the style of a 1930s opticians, this shop is a monument to all things optical. You can buy antique frames, or visit the two floors that have been turned into a museum. Pince-nez, lorgnettes, optical curiosities, star-spangled or huge retro 70s glasses, they're all here. Spec-tacular!

7 d'Theeboom

Singel, 210
☎ 623 84 20
Lunch noon-2pm, dinner 6-10pm.

The French owner of this former cheese and butter warehouse is also the chef. The menu varies according to season, with a few musts, such as cinnamon ice-cream or ice-cream with warm amarena cherries. Sheer delight!

8 Deco Sauna★

Herengracht, 115
☎ 623 82 15
Open Mon.-Thu. 10am-8pm, Fri., Sat. 11am-11pm, Sun. 1-6pm.

If you have to work up a sweat, you can at least do it in beautiful surroundings! In *Deco Sauna* every room is decorated with authentic 1920s objects. The magnificent stained glass, wood-panelling and wall and stair lamps were all bought from a large store in Paris, which was undergoing major renovation.

Antiques and bric-a-brac,
where to go and what to look for

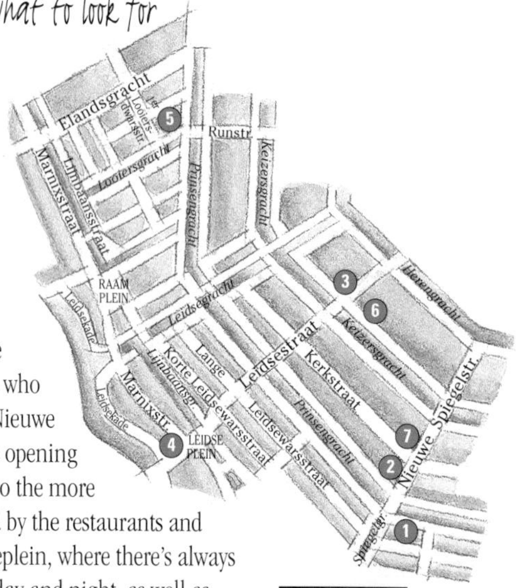

As you move from one canal to the next and from street to street, you'll find each is a little world in itself, with its own individual qualities, from the traditional, enduring values of the eighty antique dealers who have been located in Nieuwe Spiegelstraat since the opening of the Rijksmuseum, to the more basic pleasures offered by the restaurants and theatres around Leidseplein, where there's always something going on, day and night, as well as Prinsengracht, where the antique dealers find a home among the bric-a-brac shops, and are prepared to show a little originality and a sense of humour.

1 Couzijn Simon★★
Prinsengracht, 578
☎ 624 76 91
Open every day 10am-6pm.

Couzijn has two passions: his bright orange moustache and

very rare old toys. This 18th-century chemist's shop, with its floor of polished tiles, is now occupied by dolls with hair of silk thread, rocking horses, sailing boats, tea-sets for dolls' parties and clockwork dogs.

2 Frans Leidelmeijer★★
Nieuwe Spiegelstraat, 58
☎ 625 46 27
Open Tue.-Sat. 11am-6pm.

Make sure you ring the bell and take a look at the Art Nouveau and Art Deco decor

of what is, indisputably, one of the area's most beautiful antique shops. Frans Leidelmeijer, author of a book on the subject, can tell you all about the furniture and objects designed by Berlage and the Amsterdam school.

3 Metz & Co★★★

Keizersgracht, 455 (corner of Leidsestraat)
☎ 520 70 20
Open Mon.-Sat. 9.30am-6pm, Thu. 9pm, Sun. noon-5pm.

This large, very exclusive and very expensive store sells only top-of-the-range products, preferably British brands for table decoration. Every piece of furniture is signed – you might find a red and blue zig-zag chair by Rietveld for example. Under the dome by the same designer, you can have a brunch of salmon and toast, while enjoying a marvellous view of Amsterdam.

4 American Café★★

Leidsekade, 97
☎ 556 30 00
Open every day noon-10pm, Sunday brunch 2-5pm.

With the golden light pouring through its stained-glass windows, Tiffany chandeliers and lovely frescoes on the walls, this is the most authentic Art Deco setting you'll find in all Amsterdam to have a coffee or club sandwich and read the paper at the big reading table.

5 A LA PLANCHA★

Eerste Looiersdwarsstraat, 15
☎ 420 36 33
Open Tue.-Sun. noon-midnight.

If the enormous bull's head hanging behind the bar doesn't put you off, climb up onto one of the high stools to choose from the home-made tapas or grilled gambas displayed behind the glass counter. Wash it all down with rough wine to the sound of Spanish music. The temperature rises on Friday and Saturday nights, along with the sound of guitars.

6 Antiques Thom & Lenny Nelis★★

Keizersgracht, 541
☎ 623 15 46
Open Tue.-Sat. 11am-5pm.

Thom and Lenny Nelis specialise in medical antiques. Here you'll find antique medical instruments and travelling medicine chests, with well ordered little phials, some of which still contain mysterious potions. Apothecary jars and bottles line the shelves, with richly ornate painted labels from the 18th century, or decorated with paper labels from the 19th century.

7 Tribal Design★★★

Nieuwe Speigelstraat, 52
☎ 421 66 95
Open Mon.-Sat. 11am-6pm.

You could easily spend hours here, admiring the simplicity of the African chairs, the bone carvings from New Guinea, the Brazilian feather tribal dress, masks from the South Sea Islands, totems, shields, etc. A wonderful selection of primitive art in all its forms.

The museum quarter: from Rembrandt to the avant-garde

As well as being home to two of the city's most famous museums (the Museumplein is in the process of being transformed into a quiet park), this area also contains the popular Vondelpark. A haven of greenery in the heart of Amsterdam, there are trendy cafés and free concerts and shows in the open air theatre during the summer months.

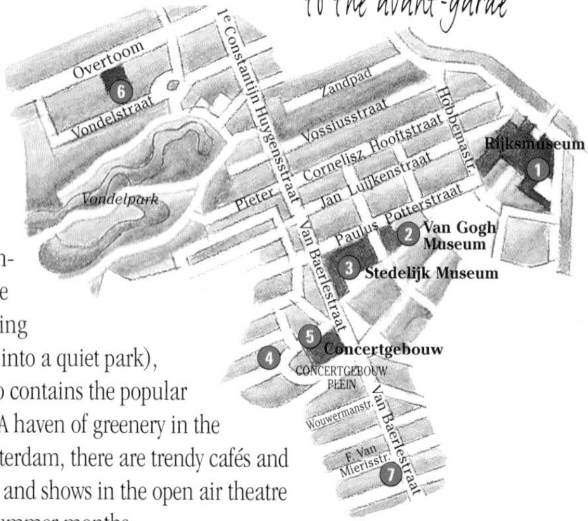

❶ National Museum★★★ *(Rijksmuseum)*

Stadhouderskade, 42
☎ 674 70 00
Entrance on south wing (department of Asiatic art), Hobbemastraat, 19
Open every day 10am-5pm
Entry charge.

This collection, with Rembrandt's *Night Watch* at its centre, is like a family

album of Dutch painting, including works by Vermeer, Frans Hals and many other masters who specialised in genre paintings, still lifes and landscapes. Don't miss the new exhibition of Asiatic art in the south wing or the exquisite collection of dolls houses *(poppenhuizen)*.

❷ Van Gogh Museum★★★

Paulus Potterstraat, 7
☎ 570 52 00
Open every day 10am-6pm
Entry charge.

This museum houses the most complete collection of this extraordinary and well-loved painter's works in the world.

Some 200 paintings and 550 sketches show Van Gogh in all his moods, from the sombre tones of *The Potato Eaters*, to the bright yellows and blues of Provence, and taken to extremes in the reds and blacks of his *Wheatfield with Crows*.

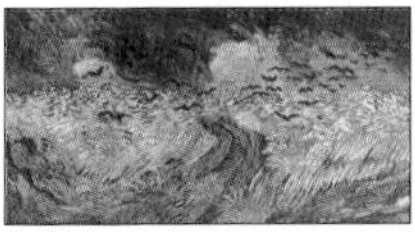

❸ City Museum★★ *(Stedelijk Museum)*

Paulus Potterstraat, 13
☎ 573 29 11
Open every day 11am-5pm, 1 Apr.-30 Sep. 10am-6pm. Entry charge.

This spacious showcase for modern and contemporary art is above all an active centre for avant-garde works. Its collections are constantly being enriched and include works by Picasso, Monet, Mondriaan, Cezanne and Chagall. It often hosts exhibitions including retrospectives and displays by young, unknown artists.

❹ Café Welling ★

J.W. Brouwersstraat, 32
☎ 662 01 55
Open 4pm-1am, Fri.-Sat. to 2am.

The pavement behind the *Concertgebouw* is filled with tables all summer long. This 'brown café', frequented by the young and trendy, is a welcome relief from the more expensive spots near by. The musicians have their own special table.

❺ Concertgebouw ★★★

Concertgebouwplein, 2-6
☎ 573 05 73
Open 10am-7pm
Concerts begin at 8.15pm.

In 1888 a new concert hall was built on piles at the heart of the residential districts, then under construction. The neo-Classical façade hides an auditorium with exceptional acoustics, which have given the *Concertgebouw* its great reputation. It is also famous for its orchestra of early instruments.

❻ Hollandse Manege★★

Vondelstraat, 140
☎ 618 09 42
Open Wed., Fri. and Sat. 10am-1pm, Sun. 10am-4pm.

Step through the heavy gate and the musky smell of working horses assails your nostrils. Based on the Spanish Riding School in Vienna, the ring has an imperial box and a metal roof, and is staggeringly large. Riders and horses have been trained here since 1882.

❼ Brasserie Van Baerle★★

Van Baerlestraat, 158
☎ 679 15 32
Open noon-11pm, Sun. from 10am, closed Sat.

The young-at-heart mingle with music-lovers in this very classy Art Deco brasserie. The shady garden is a boon in summer, as are the salads. The menu, with its hint of nouvelle cuisine, changes with the seasons. The most popular place in town for a light lunch or supper.

Plantage, dreams of far places

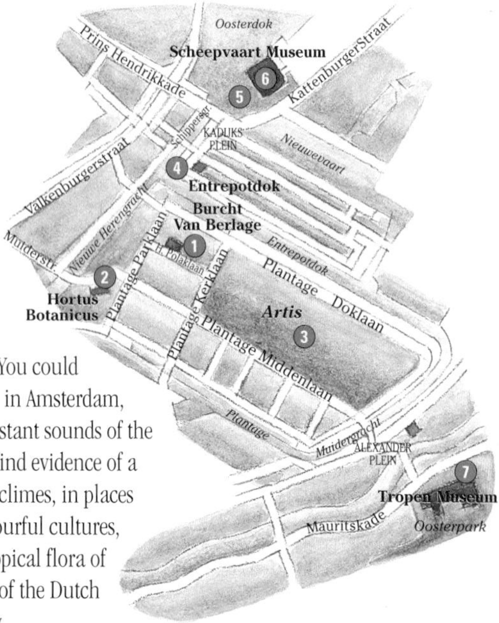

Far from the bustle of the city, elegant villas and shady avenues give this leafy district an unexpected charm. You could almost forget you're in Amsterdam, if it wasn't for the distant sounds of the city. It's here you'll find evidence of a passion for faraway climes, in places that explore the colourful cultures, exotic fauna and tropical flora of the former colonies of the Dutch East India Company.

❶ Berlage's 'Fortress'★★★ *(Burcht Van Berlage)*

Henri Polaklaan, 9
☎ 624 11 66
Open Tue.-Fri. 11am-5pm, Sun. 1-5pm
Entry charge.

The headquarters of the union of diamond-cutters and merchants is one of the finest buildings by Berlage, who designed it in 1900 in the spirit of socialism. The severity of the façade, which symbolises the strength of the workers, contrasts with the light that floods the interior, growing ever more intense as you climb the yellow stairwell, lit by a cascade of multi-faceted lamps.

❷ Hortus Botanicus★★

Plantage Middenlaan, 2a
☎ 625 84 11
Open Mon.-Fri. 9am-4pm, Sat. and Sun. 11am-4pm
Entry charge.

The V.O.C. (Dutch East India Company) first set up these wonderful tropical gardens

here in 1682 to grow medicinal herbs. Exotic plants, such as coffee and spices, were brought from the colonies and slowly acclimatised in the gardens. Don't miss the orangery, the palm house containing a four hundred-year-old cycad, and the greenhouses that maintain different climates.

3 Artis★★

Plantage Kerklaan, 40
☎ 523 34 00
Open every day 9am-5pm. Entry charge.

The city's largest park is also home to a zoo, whose many inhabitants include big cats, flamingos, polar bears and sea-lions. There's also a reptile house, an aviary with macaws and multicoloured parrots and an aquarium with tanks filled with fresh and salt water, containing over 500 species of fish and marine animals – like the ocean only smaller!

4 Entrepotdok★

Entrance on Kadijksplein.

Step through the monumental door of the Entrepotdok, head towards the end of the courtyard on the left hand side, and along the canal you'll discover an astounding array of 84 warehouses. Each bears the name of a town where the East India Company had a trading post and they are arranged in alphabetical order. The warehouses have now been converted into flats, offices and restaurants, including the *Saudade*, which serves a delicious selection of Portuguese food.

5 Aboard a V.O.C. three-master★★

The *Amsterdam*, built in 1990 and moored in front of the arsenal, is a faithful reproduction of a three-master owned by the Dutch East India Company (V.O.C.) in the 18th century. If you go aboard, you'll gain a better understanding of the physical, mental and spiritual strength required by the crew of 300 men who had to live for months, and sometimes years, in such a confined space, prey to scurvy and the elements. Not for the faint-hearted.

6 Seafaring Museum★★★ *(Scheepvaart Museum)*

Kattenburgplein, 1
☎ 523 22 22
Open Tue.-Sun. 10am-5pm, Jun.-Sep. also open Mon. Entry charge.

Relive the extraordinary adventures of the brave sailors who set forth across the seven seas, in this former Admiralty arsenal. The three floors with displays of models, navigational charts and instruments retrace the maritime history of the Netherlands. The royal launch, built in 1816 for King William III and decorated with gold leaf, is the star attraction of the exhibition.

7 Tropical Museum★★ *(Tropen Museum)*

Linnaeusstraat, 2
☎ 568 82 15
Open every day 10am-5pm Entry charge.

Beneath the glass dome of this very fine colonial building, you can travel across half the planet in less than an hour, visiting in turn the cacophony of a colourful Bombay street, the bustle of an Arab souk, or the day-to-day life of an African village. You can also find out about different types of music from around the world.

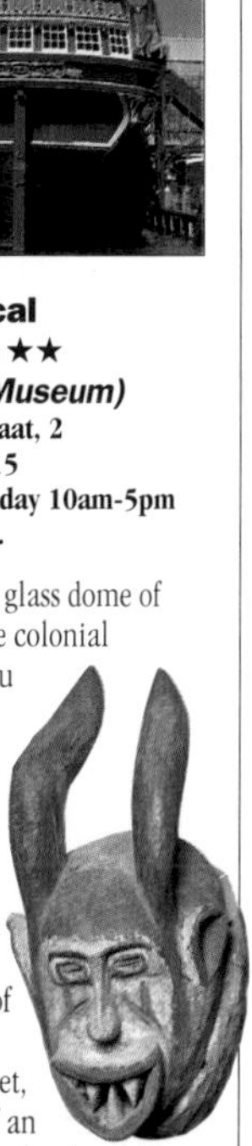

Around Centraal Station: site of the old port

Although the city of Amsterdam is built on an artificial island, the central station resolutely turns its back on the sea. Yet move away from the torrent of bicycles, trams and pedestrians trundling up to the Dam, and you'll find islands covered in warehouses, with battered old craft moored alongside.

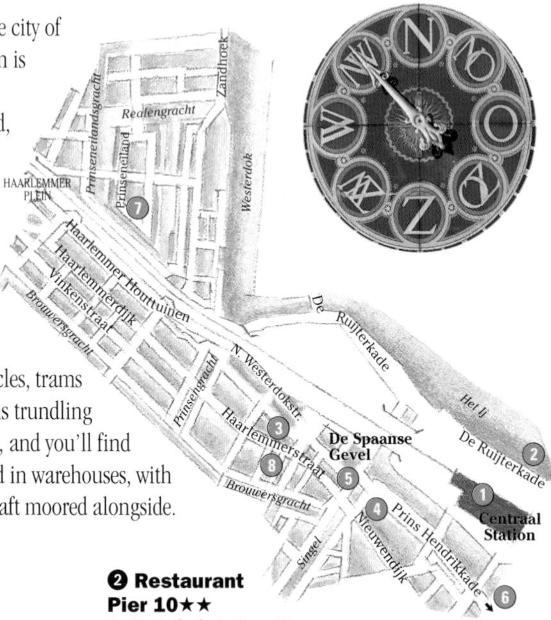

❶ Centraal Station★★

In 1869 this building, 300m/328yds long and solidly anchored in the sea by means of 8,687 piles, was a real challenge for Cuypers, the architect who designed the Rijksmuseum. Inside, on platform 2, you'll discover his secret garden, the royal waiting-room, and the *Eerste Klas* restaurant, with its Belle Époque decor.

❷ Restaurant Pier 10★★

De Ruyterkade-Steiger, 10
☎ 624 82 76
Open every day after 6.30pm (credit cards not accepted).

If you cross the central station, you'll find an old customs house, very small and apparently standing on the water, all by itself at the end of platform 10, the line to the docks. Make sure you book a

table in the rotunda, and arrive before night falls so you can enjoy the view over the port and the Ij. Generous portions and a warm, friendly ambiance.

❸ New Deli★

Haarlemmerstraat, 73
☎ 626 27 55
Open every day 9am-10pm.

Decked out in ultra-minimalist chrome and primary colours, this is where achingly hip young things come to take the weight off their Guccis and enjoy authentic Italian espresso,

7 PRINSENEILAND★

This island, far from the expensive 17th-century districts and linked to dry land by elegant draw-bridges, used to be covered in warehouses and factories that made rope and tar. When these closed the squatters moved in. It has now become a very desirable area, with its warehouses all converted to luxury flats.

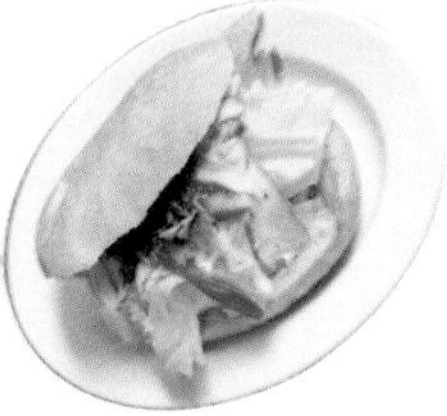

focaccia, soups, salads and Dutch rolls. Wholesome, simple food.

4 Interpolm Amsterdam

Prins Hendrikkade, 11
☎ 627 77 50
Open Mon. noon-8pm, Tue.-Fri. 9am-8pm, Sat. 9am-5pm, Sun. noon-5pm.

Want to find out all about *KC 33*, *Swiss XT* or *California Skunk*? If you're none the wiser, these are marijuana seeds, specially selected to be grown at home. Here you'll find the information, advice and equipment you need to grow this rather special plant (which is, let's not forget, illegal in most countries outside Holland).

5 The Spanish House★ *(De Spaanse Gevel)*

This café at no. 2 Singel, the canal which encircled the medieval city, has a lovely façade dated 1650, a stepped gable and a coat of arms showing a wheelbarrow. This was where the mail left for The Hague and the great merchant ships docked for unloading after passing through the lock.

6 Café 'int Aepjen'★★★

Zeedijk, 1
☎ 626 84 01
Open every day 3pm-1am, Sat. 3pm-3am.

There are only two remaining houses made from wood in Amsterdam, and this café is one of them. Built in 1521, the façade is original and the décor inside is just as sumptuous, with its paintings and panelling. The café is decorated with 17th- and 18th-century sculptures and antique liqueur bottles with beautiful painted labels.

8 West Indische Huis★

Haarlemmerstraat, 75.

This 17th-century house, with its pretty façade, was once the headquarters of the renowned West India Company (W.I.C.), not to be confused with its rival, the V.O.C. (East India Company). Today it's a municipal hall and people's university. In the central courtyard stands a statue of Peter Stuyvesant, a director of the W.I.C. who later became governor of New Amsterdam (New York).

De Pijp: a cosmopolitan atmosphere

Amsterdam has its own immigrants' quarter, located to the south of the 17th-century city. The main residents of this district are from Turkey, Morocco, Surinam or Indonesia. However, unlike immigrants to many other European capitals, they're able to coexist peacefully with the young Dutch residents, who are also drawn to the low-rent social housing schemes. The most successful of these schemes are undoubtedly those designed in the 1920s by architects from the Amsterdam school. Elsewhere narrow streets and cramped houses have earned this district the unflattering name of 'pipe' *(pijp)*.

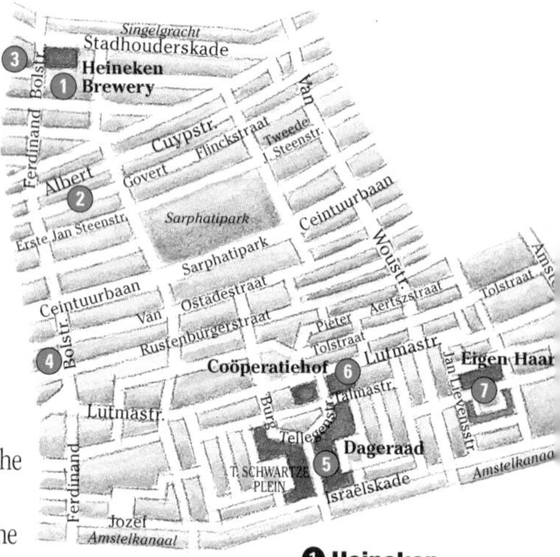

❶ Heineken Brewery★★

Stadhouderskade, 78 (corner of F. Bolstraat)
☎ 523 96 66
Guided tours Mon.-Fri. 9.30am, 11am, 1pm and 2.30pm, Sat. in Jul. and Aug. Entry charge.

The most famous of the Dutch breweries has moved to a more modern factory, but the old building has been converted into a beer museum. It's just been renovated and updated, with a little help from the Internet, and now offers an interactive tour of the history of beer and the Heineken brewery. When you've worked up a good thirst, there's a tasting session too.

❷ Albert Cuypmarkt★

Albert Cuypstraat
Open Mon.-Sat. 10am-4.30pm.

Since 1905 this has been the most frequented, popular and

cosmopolitan of the city's markets. It has around three hundred stalls stretching for 2km/1 mile, selling clothing, fabrics by the metre, fish, cheese, flowers, fruit and vegetables, all at very low prices.

'Amsterdam, Turkish, Christian, Pagan, Jewish. Reservoir of sects and crucible of schisms, this bank of conscience where every opinion, however strange, is given credit and value.'

Marwell

❸ De Taart Van M'n Tante★

1e Jacob van Campenstraat, 35
☎ 776 46 00
Open Mon.-Sat. 9am-5pm (best to phone in advance).

Everything is for sale in this huge warehouse hidden behind the stallholders' displays – rustic wardrobes, large mirrors, display cases, mahogany writing desks, Chinese boxes, knick-knacks and ice-skates, all for really good prices. If you look very carefully you're bound to find some rare treasure.

❹ Gambrinus★

Ferdinand Bolstraat, 180
☎ 671 73 89
Open every day 11am-1pm, Fri.-Sat. 11am-2am, kitchen open 6-10pm.

This little 'brown café' gets very lively after 6pm, and offers good French, English and Italian food, as well as hearty soups, Dutch sandwiches and apple pie.

❺ Dageraad★★★

P L Takstraat.

In 1921 a socialist building cooperative asked two architects, M de Klerk and P L Kramer, to draw up plans for 350 workers' housing units. The two brick buildings on the corner of P L Takstraat sum up the philosophy of the Amsterdam school, which advocated rigour, verticality and colour in designs combining utilitarianism with beauty.

❻ Coöperatiehof★

Entrance on Talmastraat.

In the Dutch tradition of the *hof*, a kind of courtyard surrounded by housing for the needy, this symmetrical group is dominated not by a church but by the bell tower of the public library. The books and key on the façade symbolise the emancipation of the working class through knowledge.

❼ Eigen Haard★★

Smaragdplein.

Another remarkable social housing scheme designed by the Amsterdam school for the Eigen Haard (Home) cooperative in 1917. The school and housing units are all symmetrical in design. This formalism is offset by the use of soft-toned building materials, and, in places, decorative brickwork.

Rooms and restaurants
Practicalities

Amsterdam is comparatively small, so your main concerns when choosing a hotel will be price and location. Avoid the central station area and the red light district unless you like noise and unsavoury characters. The hotels outside these two areas are easy to get to by tram or taxi, or even on foot, if you aren't too heavily loaded.

HOTELS

The luxury hotels have reduced rates at weekends, particularly if you book through a travel agent, although this may mean you don't get such a good room. There are also many very quiet and comfortable hotels near Vondelpark. The (very large) breakfast is usually included in the price. Low season prices apply from the end of November to the end of April, and also in July and August.

You're not usually expected to leave a tip, unless you're staying in a luxury hotel, where you should tip messenger boys and chambermaids.

Hotels in Amsterdam are classified according to international standards. There's an enormous amount of choice; however you should remember that a hotel's star rating is based on objective criteria, such as whether or not it has a lift, or televisions in the rooms. So in the 2 and 3 star categories, you'll find excellent old-style hotels in former patrician houses, where the atmosphere tends to be warmer and more welcoming. These are the hotels we prefer to recommend.

> **BOOKING A HOTEL**
>
> These days it's best to plan ahead and pre-book your hotel in Amsterdam. You can call the Amsterdam Reservations Centre (☎ 00 31 777 000 888, open Mon.-Fri. 9am-5pm), a central booking service where you'll be dealt with by someone who speaks English. You can also e-mail your booking to: reservations@amsterdamtourist.nl You can also book directly on the internet with a credit card. Try a booking service such as www.octopustravel.com where you will be able to compare prices and facilities to help you decide.

In you're going in spring – particularly April or May – or September, it's a good idea to book several weeks in advance. This is even more important if you've chosen a nice little old-style hotel with a view of the canal. You can book by telephone or fax using a credit card – don't forget to include your address and card number when booking by fax. Postal orders and eurocheques are also accepted for payment. If you fail to take up your reservation, you'll be charged a cancellation fee corresponding to the price of one night at the hotel.

Restaurants

The Dutch like to economise and don't often eat out. Restaurants are generally the preserve of businessmen and tourists and can be very expensive if you pick from the à la carte menu. For this reason, the great majority of restaurants offer more reasonably-priced set meals of between 3 and 5 courses.

Prices as shown include a 15% service charge. The Dutch seldom leave a tip, though they may round up the bill to the nearest euro or ten euros. If you do feel you want to leave a tip in a restaurant, you shouldn't make it more than €5.

Lastly, remember that the Dutch eat early. Restaurants are open from 6pm and the kitchen usually closes at 10pm. A few places around the *Concertgebouw*, Leidseplein and Rembrandtplein stay open until midnight. However the most sensible thing is always to call first and book if you want to make sure you don't wind up in McDonald's. Our selections are largely based on value for money.

Typical dishes

Typical Dutch food is sturdy winter food, like *stamppot*: mashed potato mixed with vegetables (cabbage or endive) and meat, often fried bacon or minced meat. Another national dish is the Dutch pancake (sweet or savoury fillings), which is so filling that you can eat it as a meal. Most restaurants nowadays serve 'modern' food; a combination of cuisines from all over the world. There are some old fashioned restaurants that serve traditional Dutch food, but they are mostly visited by tourists. Those showing the *Neerlands Dis* logo all serve traditional cuisine. All these restaurants will have an English version of their menu. Indonesian food is very popular in Holland since Indonesia was once a Dutch colony.

Active or passive smoking?

As yet, there is no anti-smoking legislation in the Netherlands, which means that very few restaurants or cafés have no-smoking zones.

In cafés you can often order snacks like a cheese platter, *vlammetjes* or *bitterballen*. *Jenever* (Dutch version of gin) is the national drink. A late night favourite is 'eating out of the wall' in brightly lit snack bars called *Febo* where the deep fried snacks are displayed and kept hot in individual vending machines. During the day, you can eat on the street at various fish stalls where you can try the famous raw herring or other smoked or fried fish. See page 125 for a list of other Dutch dishes and tips on understanding the menu.

HOTELS

Near the Béguinage

Estheréa★★★

Singel, 303-309
☎ 624 51 46
Ⓕ 623 90 01
Trams 1, 2, 5.

Four old brick buildings near the flower market, renovated and very pretty. The breakfast room is decorated in dark shades, with typical Dutch wood panelling and the bedrooms are large and comfortable.

Near Leidseplein

American★★★★

Leidsekade, 97
☎ 556 30 00
Ⓕ 556 30 01
Trams 1, 2, 5, 11.

In the early 20th century the decor of this hotel, where Mata Hari consummated her eighth marriage, was pure Art Nouveau. Although the original decoration has gone from the pastel bedrooms with their large bathrooms, the famous Art Deco American Café is still *the* meeting-place for Amsterdam's intellectuals. The hotel has terraces on Leidseplein and, on the top floor, a fitness centre and 8-space car park.

Dikker & Thiys ★★★

Prinsengracht, 444
☎ 620 12 12
Ⓕ 625 89 86
Trams 1, 2, 5, 11.

A luxury establishment a stone's throw from Leidseplein. Unfortunately, recent restoration has removed all its Art Deco elements. Decorated in greys and pinks, with large bathrooms and one of Amsterdam's really good restaurants, the *Prinsenkelder*, in the basement. There's a car park (not free) 100m/yds away. The bedrooms overlooking Prinsengracht are quieter.

The flower-filled courtyard of the Pulitzer hotel

Near Rembrandtplein

Seven Bridges★★

Reguliersgracht, 3
☎ 623 13 29
Tram 4.

A small, 8-room hotel by the most beautiful of the canals, whose owner, a secondhand dealer, has decorated it in a range of styles, from empire to Art Deco. Vases filled with flowers, Persian carpets and a big breakfast served in bed. Views over the garden or the canal, but the staircase is steep. An excellent hotel.

Prinsenhof★

Prinsengracht, 810
☎ 623 17 72
Ⓕ 638 33 68
Tram 4.

Small, tastefully-decorated hotel near Frederiksplein and the friendly cafés of Utrechtsestraat, which would suit those on limited budgets who don't mind steep stairs. Book in advance if you want one of the 2 bedrooms with an en-suite shower. 5% additional charge for credit cards.

Jordaan

Pulitzer★★★★★

Prinsengracht, 315-331
☎ 523 52 35
Ⓕ 627 67 53
Trams 13, 14, 17.

Views of the canal or the courtyard garden of this unusual hotel occupying a block of 27

bourgeois residences between Prinsengracht and Keizersgracht. Clients generally businessmen and conference participants. Good location close to Jordaan. Inexpensive nouvelle cuisine in the *Café Pulitzer* and the gourmet restaurant in a former chemist's shop, *De Goudsbloem*. For real style, arrive by boat.

Canal House★★★

Keizersgracht, 148
☎ 622 51 82 Ⓕ 624 13 17.
Trams 13, 17.

The best-designed of the small, old-style hotels. Intimate 17th-century decor in a beautiful house on the edge of Jordaan. Crystal chandeliers, freshly-cut flowers, period furniture and antiques. Book two months in advance.

Toren★★★

Keizersgracht, 164
☎ 622 63 52
Ⓕ 626 97 05
Trams 13, 17.

Situated on one of the most beautiful canals, this hotel is comfortable and welcoming. Ask for a room overlooking either the canal or the small, Laura Ashley-style house in the garden (room 111). Special offers for three nights during the winter. Characterful bar with old woodwork.

Acacia★

Lindengracht, 251
☎ 622 14 60
Ⓕ 638 07 48
www.hotelacacia.nl

A small hotel with 14 rooms and a very Dutch feel, run by a young couple. En-suite bathrooms in every room and a large breakfast included in the price. For something different, try one of the rooms in the hotel's two houseboats on the nearby canal. Very popular, so booking is a must. Add 5% to the bill for payment by credit card.

Herengracht

Ambassade★★★

Herengracht, 341
☎ 555 02 22
Ⓕ 555 02 77
Trams 1, 2, 5.

The favourite hotel of authors Michel Tournier and Umberto Eco, this is the most luxurious of the old-style hotels, occupying eight fine 17th-century houses. Period furniture and interesting and unusual decor in the public areas. A choice of top-floor bedrooms under the rafters or very large rooms overlooking the canal. So quiet you can hear the ducks quacking. Twenty-four-hour restaurant service.

The Ambassade hotel on Herengracht.

Keizershof★

Keizersgracht, 618
☎ 622 28 55
Ⓕ 624 84 12
Trams 16, 24, 25.

An authentic 17th-century building, where Mrs de Vries makes you feel at home in a typically Dutch setting. Six pleasant rooms with period furniture and old-fashioned linen. In good weather breakfast is served in the flower-filled garden and there's a piano in the sitting-room.

Plantage

Amstel Inter-Continental ★★★★★

Prof. Tulpplein, 1
☎ 622 60 60
Ⓕ 622 58 08
Metro Weesperplein or trams 6, 7, 10.

This luxury hotel, built in 1867 and restored at great expense, offers its clients a personalised service. The 79 rooms are full of surprises, from expensive furniture and silk sheets to crystal carafes in the bar and a bathroom fit for a film star. Other features include supervised parking, heated pool, sauna, Turkish bath, limousines and gourmet restaurant, *La Rive*, with its terrace by the Amstel.

Near Centraal Station

New York★★

Herengracht, 13
☎ 624 30 66
Ⓕ 620 32 30.

At the northern end of Herengracht and a stone's throw from the central station. Popular with both gay men and women. Very modern and clean, with marble and mirrors on every floor. Small private garage. Breakfast times to cater for late risers.

Rokin

De L'Europe ★★★★★

Nieuwe Doelenstraat, 2-8
☎ 531 17 77
Ⓕ 531 17 78
Trams 4, 9, 14, 16, 24, 25.

This luxury hotel, with its great location in the heart of Amsterdam, was opened in 1896 and recently celebrated its centenary. Famous guests have included Elizabeth Taylor. The hotel combines refinement with personalised service and has an excellent restaurant, the *Excelsior*, a large waterside terrace, a fitness centre with a small, Hollywood-style swimming pool and a private car park. Ask for a room with a balcony overlooking the Amstel.

Agora★

Singel, 462
☎ 627 22 00
Ⓕ 627 22 02
Trams 4, 9, 14, 16, 24, 25.

This old building near the flower market has been nicely restored by two friends. The rooms overlooking the canal are noisier, though more expensive. A lovely setting for breakfast.

The museum quarter

Jan Luyken★★★★

Jan Luykenstraat, 58
☎ 573 07 30
Ⓕ 676 38 41
Trams 2, 3, 5, 12.

Jan Luyken
HOTEL & RESIDENCE
★ ★ ★ ★

In a quiet street near Vondelpark, theatres and museums, the van Schaik family have turned three 19th-century patrician houses into a hotel. Quiet atmosphere, classic furniture, Art Nouveau decor and a warm welcome at an affordable price. Street parking possible but not free.

Toro★★★

Koningslaan, 64.
☎ 673 72 23
Ⓕ 675 00 31
Tram 2.

An old patrician house 10 mins from the centre, next to Vondelpark, with 22 comfortable and deliciously quiet rooms. Features include a breakfast room open to the garden, terrace, antique furniture, oriental carpets and a warm welcome. There are many parking facilities available in the area. Excellent value for money.

Villa Borgmann★★

Koningslaan, 48
☎ 673 52 52
Ⓕ 676 25 80
Tram 2.

This small, peaceful and welcoming hotel, situated in the residential area by Vondelpark, has 15 rooms with en-suite showers, the best of which overlook the park. Furnished in cane and pastel tones. Parking available nearby.

De Filosoof★★

Anna Vodelstraat, 6
☎ 683 30 13
Ⓕ 685 37 50.

This hotel near Vondelpark and the cinema museum has an unusual feature – the decor in each of its 25 rooms is based on a philosopher. You sleep under the watchful eye of Kant, Goethe, Marx, Dante or one of the great Japanese thinkers. Not that this means a lack of comfort – quite the opposite in fact. Breakfast in the garden in fine weather. A quality address.

The Toro hotel, amidst the greenery of the Vondelpark

Restaurants

Near the Béguinage

KANTJIL

Kantjil & De Tijger★★

Spuistraat, 291-293
☎ 620 09 94
Trams 1, 2, 5
Open every day after 4.30pm.

A very fashionable Indonesian restaurant, despite unexciting decor. Serves many Javanese specialities, as well as the inevitable and very copious *rijsttafel*.

Haesje Claes★★

Spuitraat, 275
☎ 624 99 98
Trams 1, 2, 5
Open every day noon-10pm.

This restaurant sports the *Neerlands Dis* sign, indicating a typical Dutch establishment. Inside simple food is served in a warm and friendly atmosphere.

DE ROODE LEEUW
HOTEL·RESTAURANT·BRASSERIE

The *hollandse visbord,* an assortment of herring, mackerel, shrimps and smoked eels, is a house speciality.

Dam

De Roode Leeuw ★★

Damrak, 93-94
☎ 555 06 66.
Open every day noon-10pm.

A traditional brasserie serving Dutch meat and fish specialities. Vegetables in season – particularly asparagus – are cooked in a great variety of ways. Covered terrace on the busy Damrak.

Red light district

Hemelse Modder ★★

Oude Waal, 11
☎ 624 32 03
Bus 22
Open every day except Mon. 6pm-1am

Indian, Italian, French and vegetarian dishes, tending towards nouvelle cuisine, are served in a simple setting overlooking the quiet canal. Three-course set meal at around €24. Restaurant run by former squatters who know how to cook. Very popular, so booking a must.

Wellcome★

Zeedijk, 57
☎ 638 62 34
Bus 22
Open every day noon-11pm

The district's best Chinese restaurant specialising in very fresh seafood. Pleasant ambiance and chef's surprises, such as grilled oysters and steamed scallops.

Jordaan

Long Pura★★★

Rozengracht, 46-48
☎ 623 89 50
Trams 13, 14, 17
Open every day 6-11pm.

Sublime decor of richly-coloured fabrics through which

actor-waiters glide. Serves authentic Balinese cuisine, subtle and delicate, from *Makanan Nusantara* to stuffed duck with Indonesian spices.

Bordewijk★★★

Noordermarkt, 7
☎ 624 38 99
Open evenings only.
Closed Mon.

High-tech decor and background music, excellent cuisine varying according to what is on sale in the market at the time, with fish and game specialities. Booking a must for this very popular restaurant known for its wines.

De Bak★

Prinsengracht, 193 (near Prinsenstraat)
☎ 625 79 72
Open every day 5-11pm.

Odd and very friendly – the basement of an old canal house transformed into a restaurant-car. Those who like good meat cooked on a charcoal grill should be sure not to miss this one. New set meal every day at €11.

Toscanini★★

Lindengracht, 75
☎ 623 28 13
Tram 10.
Open every day except Sun. after 6pm. Booking advisable.

De Bak

A converted factory boasting a beautiful interior decor and a female chef. Inexpensive gourmet dishes are cooked using fresh produce, the wine list is interesting and the atmosphere very warm and lively.

Jewish quarter

De Magere Brug★

Amstel, 81
☎ 622 65 02
Metro Waterlooplein.
Open every day from noon.
Kitchen closes at 9pm.

Small, unpretentious restaurant with a terrace opposite the *Magere Brug* ('Thin Bridge') over the Amstel. Particularly popular with Amsterdamers because of its home cooking at good prices. Snails, spare-ribs and veal liver are served along with herrings, eels and shrimps.

Rokin

Tom Yam★★

Staalstraat, 22
☎ 622 95 33
Trams 4, 9, 16, 24, 25
Open Tue.-Sat. from 6pm.

Perfect service in a pleasing decor. The Thai cuisine has all the subtle flavours of citronella and coriander and is sometimes also very hot and spicy. Set meals from €18, but for a minimum of two people only. Beware – the wines are very expensive!

Near Rembrandtplein

Sichuan Food ★★★★

Reguliersdwarsstraat, 35
☎ 626 93 27
Trams 16, 24, 25
Open every day 5.30pm-2am.

Authentic Chinese cuisine awarded stars by the gourmet guides. You must try this place, particularly the hot and spicy Sichuan specialities. Ask the owner to compose a meal for you, but expect to pay highly for it!

Indonesisch Restaurant Tempo Doeloe★★★

Utrechtsestraat, 75
☎ 625 67 18
Open every day 6-11.30pm.

You must try the grilled tiger prawns in coconut curry sauce, the most popular dish on the menu. Set meals start at €22.25 and the menu tells you how spicy each dish will be. If you'd like to try out the hottest ones, and need some advice, just ask!

Le Pêcheur★★

Regulierdwarsstraat, 32
☎ 624 31 21
Trams 16, 24, 25
Open Mon.-Fri. noon-2.30pm and 6-10.30pm, Sat. dinner only

A fine selection of fish and other seafood cooked the Italian way in a former shed. *Sashimi*, caviar, oyster and lobster snacks served until 1am. Eat in the garden in summer.

Near Leidseplein

Prinsenkelder★★★

Prinsengracht, 438
☎ 422 27 77
Trams 1, 2, 5, 11
Open Tue.-Sat. from 6pm.

Cellar with an intimate atmosphere and sober black and white decor enlivened by exotic wood and large bouquets of flowers. Generous portions of imaginative Franco-Italian cuisine, accompanied by wines selected in France, Italy, Australia and South Africa. Not be be missed!

Bento★★

Kerkstraat, 148
☎ 622 42 48
Trams 16, 24, 25
Open 5.30-10pm, except Mon.

Very Japanese decor of tatami mats and bamboo in which to eat healthy, balanced food served on appropriate dishes. Raw and cooked fish as well as vegetarian food.

Near Herengracht

Christophe★★★★

Leliegracht, 46
☎ 625 08 07
Trams 13, 14, 17
Open Tue.-Sat. after 6.30pm.

Classic cuisine from south-west France, reinvented by French chef Jean-Christophe Royer. Very unusual decor by Dutch designer Paul van den Berg. Excellent wine list.

't Heertje★★

Herenstraat, 16
☎ 625 81 27
Trams 1, 2, 5
Open Thu.-Mon. from 5.30pm.

Not a wide choice, but the menu of subtle, imaginative cuisine changes daily, depending on the

produce available at the fishmonger's opposite. Traditional food also served. Only 8 tables, so it's best to book in advance.

Zest★★★

Orubsebstraatn, 10
☎ 428 24 66
Open Mon.-Sat, 5.30-11.30pm.

Cosy restaurant with light, sophisticated cuisine at reasonable prices (starters around €11, main courses €20). Simple, elegant décor. Very welcoming. Booking advisable at weekends.

The museum quarter

Bodega Keyzer ★★★

Van Baerlestraat, 96
☎ 671 14 81
Trams 3, 12
Open noon-11 pm.

Classy diner favoured by musicians and music lovers from the *Concertgebouw*. The best sole meunière in town and a delicious fruit zabaglione. Booking essential.

Le Garage★★★

Ruysdaelstraat, 54-56
☎ 679 71 76
Trams 3, 5, 12
Open Mon.-Fri. noon-2pm, 6-11pm, Sat. and Sun. dinner only.

Very fashionable. A garage transformed by the architect of the Stopera, frequented by those in the know. Red benches and mirrors where you can nibble at the slimming menu or try a few supposedly French specialities. In other words, the food isn't the main attraction. Booking essential.

Sama Sebo★★

P.C. Hoofstraat, 27
☎ 662 81 46
Bus 63
Open noon-10pm, closed Sun.

Affordable *nasi goreng* and *bami goreng* specialities and 23-dish *rijsttafel* near the Rijksmuseum. Very welcoming with pleasant decor.

Zabar's★★

Van Baerlestraat, 49
☎ 679 88 88
Trams 3, 5, 12
Open 11am-1am, closed Sun. Dinner only Mon. and Sat.

Pretty interior open to a garden decorated in trompe-l'œil. Mediterranean cuisine for the

greedy. A choice of *gazpacho*, *zarzuela*, *tajines* or *carpaccio* with delicious desserts. Mixed, but generally younger clientele.

Near Centraal Station

De Silveren Spiegel★★★

Kattengat, 4-6
☎ 624 65 89
Dinner from 6pm, not Sun.

Candlelit decor in 17th-century house. Warm welcome and highly inventive cuisine from starter to dessert, created by a gourmet chef who loves good French wines. Very affordable prices for one of Amsterdam's best restaurants. Booking advisable.

Eerste Klas★★

Stationplein, 15
☎ 625 01 31
Open 9.30am-11pm, dinner 5-10pm

An oasis of peace amidst the hustle and bustle of the station. Next to the gilded gate of the Queen's waiting-room on platform 2B, the Four Seasons Saloon has been transformed into a superb brasserie serving traditional cuisine à la carte. *Fin de siècle* atmosphere.

LIGHT MEALS AND SNACKS

The Pancake Bakery

Prinsengracht, 191
☎ 625 13 33
Open noon-9.30pm.

If it's generous portions at great prices you're after, here you can choose from 40 kinds of savoury and sweet pancakes. There are some unusual taste combinations, such as the cheese and ginger pancake. It's always packed, so expect to wait.

Caffe Esprit

Spui, 10A
☎ 622 19 67
Open Mon.-Sat. 10am-6pm, Thu. until 10pm, Sun. noon-6pm.

Formerly known as 'Oibibio', this café-restaurant is located on the first floor of the old Hotel Mercurius near the central station. Here you'll find a Japanese teahouse where you can sip your tea in a timeless atmosphere.

CAFÉ PRACTICALITIES

If you sit out on the terrace, you'll be asked to pay immediately. Inside the 'brown cafés' the waiter will keep a record of what you have in his notebook. Over an evening, and lulled by a few *jenevers*, you can find yourself running up a sizable bill. You have been warned!

Café Pulitzer

Prinsengracht, 315-331
☎ 523 52 35
Open 24 hours every day.

A chic eatery where you can try the dish of the day or just have a cup of tea and a delicious pastry.

Small Talk

Van Baerlestraat, 52
☎ 671 48 64
Open Mon.-Fri. 10am-9,30pm, Sat. and Sun. until 8.30pm.

In the chic part of town, very good tarts made on the premises and a good selection of teas. The terrace is rather noisy.

CAFÉS

Café Chris

Bloemstraat, 42
☎ 624 59 42
Mon.-Sat. 2pm-1am.

Situated in Jordaan, near Westerkerk, this historic 'brown café' (1624) is a popular student haunt.

De Druif

Rapenburgerplein, 83
☎ 624 45 30 (near the Seafaring Museum)
Open every day 11am-1am.

A truly authentic Amsterdam café housed in a former *jenever* distillery, far from the tourist circuit in the former dockland area.

Het Molenpad

Prinsengracht, 653
☎ 625 96 80
Open every day noon-1am.

Photographic exhibitions and a very literary clientele in this lovely 'brown café'. Try some delicious *bitterballen* with your beer.

De Blincker

St Barberenstraat, 7
☎ 627 19 38
Open Mon.-Sat. from 6pm.

Near the avant-garde theatres, a very trendy bar with a fine high-tech decor and a winter garden open in the late afternoon.

Luxembourg

Spui, 22-24
☎ 620 62 64
Open every day 9am-1am.

Marble, copper and polished wood set a tone of old-fashioned comfort. A meeting- place for the young and hip, with yuppies and media people after 5pm.

Spanjer van Twist

Leliegracht, 60
☎ 639 01 09.

Café overlooking a lovely shady canal, with tables set up outside as soon as the sun shines. The patrons tend to be young and resolutely non-conformist. Snacks and light meals served all day.

Finch

Noordermarkt, 5
☎ 626 24 61
Open every day 11am-1am, Sat. to 2am.

A pleasant little bistrot where the locals come to sip a glass of wine after the Saturday market or to enjoy the dish of the day.

THE *PROEFLOKAAL*

A *proeflokaal* is a bar where you drink *jenever*. Originally these places were attached to breweries. Inside you'll find a wide range of beers as well as spirits. Usually open from 11am-8pm.

De Admiraal

Herengracht, 319
☎ 625 43 34
Open Mon.-Sat. 4.30-11pm.

Rustic decor with barrels piled up to the ceiling and wooden tables where you can enjoy a candlelit dinner or try the *jenevers* made by van Wees, the oldest distillery in Jordaan.

De Ooievaar

Sint Olofspoort, 1 (corner of Zeedijk)
☎ 420 80 04
Open Mon.-Fri. 3pm-1am, Sat., Sun. 1pm-1am.

The building housing this venerable institution tilts a little because of its age (1620), and not because you've drunk too many little frosted glasses of highly-flavoured *oud*. This *proeflokaal* dedicated to the stork is one of the oldest and most pleasant of them all.

Het Proeflokaal

Pijlsteeg, 31
☎ 639 26 95
Open every day 3-9pm.

The old Wyn and Fockink distillery founded in 1679 has reopened in an alleyway behind the Dam. Here you can sample both its own products and other brands of liqueur and *jenever* in a very cosy atmosphere.

In de Wildeman

Kolksteeg, 3
☎ 638 23 48
Open every day noon-1am.

A lovely place near the station and the red light district. The decor looks like an interior in a Dutch painting, with its copper chandeliers, wood panelling and black and white tiled floor. A choice of 150 types of beer, including 18 on draught.

A
B
1
2
3
Noorderkerk
Westerkerk
Westermarkt
Magna Plazza
Nieuwe Kerk
DAM
Koninklijk Paleis
Begijnhof
Spui
KONINGSPL.
MUNT PLEIN
RAAMPL.
LEIDSEPLEIN
Van Loon Museum
Rijksmuseum
Van Gogh Museum
Stedelijk Museum
Heineken Brouwerij
Vondelpark
Frederik Hendrik Plantsoen
Prinsenhof
Haarlemmerdijk
Vinkenstraat
Brouwersgracht
Nieuwe Westerdokstraat
Haarlemmerstraat
Brouwersgr.
De Wittenkade
De Wittenstraat
Van Beuningenstraat
Jacob Catskade
Nassaukade
Marnixkade
Marnixstraat
Van Hallstraat
Fagelstraat
Palmgr.
Palmstraat
Willemsstraat
Goudsbloemstraat
Lindengracht
Lindenstraat
Boomstr.
Tichelstr.
Lijnbaansgracht
Westerstraat
Anjeliersstraat
Tuinstraat
Egelantiersstraat
Egelantiersgracht
Nieuwe Leliestraat
Leliegracht
Bloemgracht
Bloemstraat
Rozengracht
Rozenstraat
Lauriersstraat
Lauriergracht
Elandsstraat
Elandsgracht
Runstr.
Huidenstr.
Looiersgr.
Passeerdersgr.
Leidsegracht
Prinsengracht
Keizersgracht
Herengracht
Singel
Spuistraat
Nieuwezijds Voorburgwal
Raadhuisstraat
Damrak
Warmoesstraat
Damstr.
Nes
Rokin
Kalverstraat
Oudezijds
Nieuwendijk
Beurs
Heiligeweg
Nieuwe Doelenstr.
Reguliersbreestraat
Reguliersdwarsstraat
Herengr.
Leidsestraat
Kerkstraat
Nieuwe Spiegelstr.
Vijzelstraat
Lange
Korte
Leidsedwarsstraat
Leidsedwarsstr.
Spiegelgr.
Weteringschans
Stadhouderskade
Vijzelgracht
Noorderstraat
Nieuwe Looiersstr.
Lijnbaansgracht
Den Texstraat
Nicolaas
Reguliersgracht
G. van Ledenberchstr.
Hogerbeetsstr.
Rombout
Hendrikstraat
Oldenbarneveldstr.
Frederik
Van
H. de Grootkade
De Clercqstraat
Da Costakade
Da Costastraat
Potgieterstraat
Bilderdijkstraat
Kinkerstraat
Jacob Van Lennepstraat
Lennepkade
Jacob Van Lennepkade
J. Van Lennepkade
Bosboom Toussaintstr.
Derde Helmersstraat
Helmersstraat
Tweede C. Huygensstraat
1e Tweede
Helmersstraat
Erste
Overtoom
Vondelstraat
Constantijn Huygensstraat
Vondelstr.
Zandpad
Vossiusstraat
Hobbemastr.
Cornelisz Hooftstr.
Pieter
Luijkenstr.
Jan
Paulus Potterstr.
Van Eeghenlaan
Van Eeghenstraat
Van Baerlestr.
Willemsparkweg
Vermeerstr.
Hobbemakade
Ruysdaelkade
1e J. Van Campenstr.
F. Bolstr.

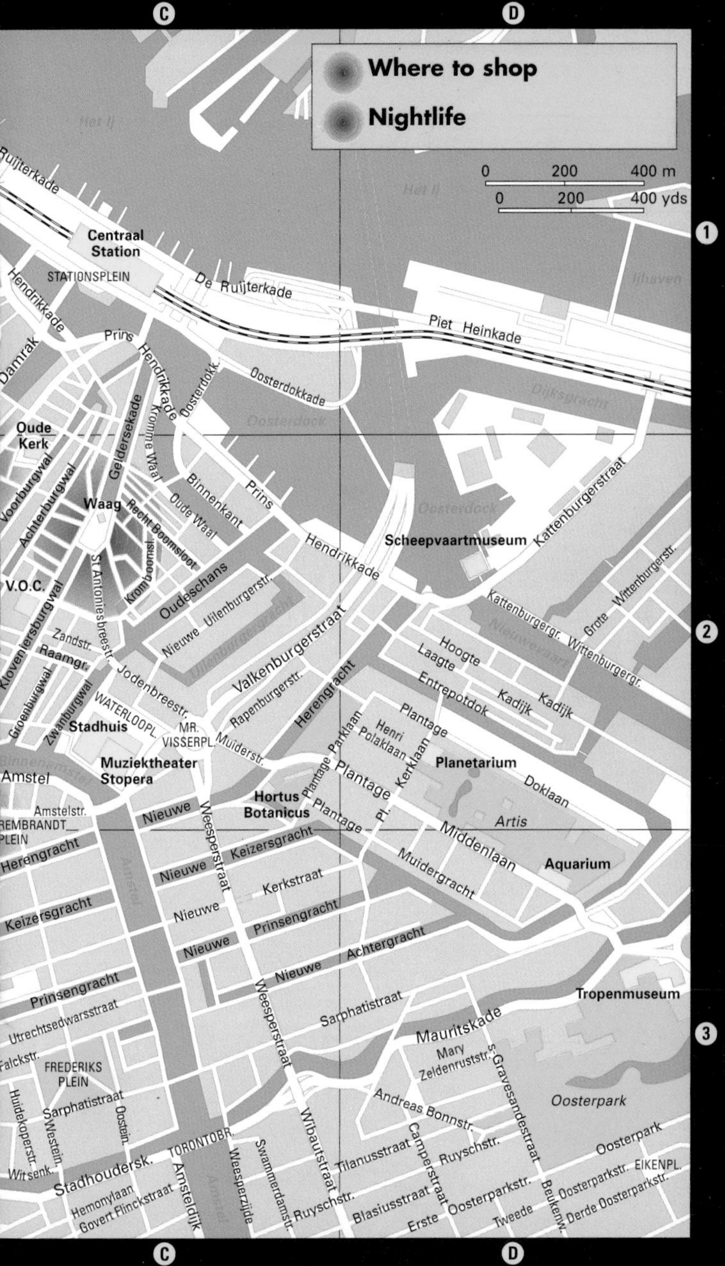
C
D
Where to shop
Nightlife
0 200 400 m
0 200 400 yds
1
2
3
Het IJ
IJhaven
Ruijterkade
Centraal Station
STATIONSPLEIN
De Ruijterkade
Piet Heinkade
Hendrikkade
Prins Hendrikkade
Damrak
Oosterdokk.
Oosterdokkade
Oosterdock
Dijksgracht
Oude Kerk
Geldersekade
Kromme Waal
Voorburgwal
Achterburgwal
Waag
Binnenkant
Oude Waal
Recht Boomsloot
Scheepvaartmuseum
Kattenburgerstraat
V.O.C.
St Antoniesbreestr.
Kromboomsl.
Oudeschans
Nieuwe Uilenburgerstr.
Uilenburgergracht
Kloveniersburgwal
Zandstr.
Raamgr.
Jodenbreestr.
Valkenburgerstraat
Rapenburgerstr.
Herengracht
Kattenburgergr.
Grote Wittenburgerstr.
Wittenburgergr.
Nieuwevaart
Hoogte Kadijk
Laagte Kadijk
Entrepotdok
Groenburgwal
Zwanburgwal
WATERLOOPL.
Stadhuis
MR. VISSERPL.
Muiderstr.
Plantage Parklaan
Henri Polaklaan
Plantage Kerklaan
Planetarium
Binnenamstel
Amstel
Muziektheater Stopera
Hortus Botanicus
Plantage
Plantage Doklaan
Amstelstr.
REMBRANDT PLEIN
Nieuwe
Weesperstraat
Plantage Middenlaan
Artis
Aquarium
Herengracht
Keizersgracht
Nieuwe Keizersgracht
Kerkstraat
Muidergracht
Nieuwe
Prinsengracht
Nieuwe Prinsengracht
Nieuwe Achtergracht
Keizersgracht
Amstel
Prinsengracht
Utrechtsedwarsstraat
Sarphatistraat
Tropenmuseum
Mauritskade
Falckstr.
FREDERIKS PLEIN
Mary Zeldenruststr.
's-Gravesandestraat
Oosterpark
Huidekoperstr.
Westein.
Sarphatistraat
Oostein.
Andreas Bonnstr.
Witsenk.
Stadhoudersk.
TORONTOBR.
Weesperzijde
Swammerdamstr.
Wibautstraat
Camperstraat
Ruyschstr.
Tilanusstraat
Oosterpark
Hemonylaan
Govert Flinckstraat
Amsteldijk
Ruyschstr.
Blasiusstraat
Erste Oosterparkstr.
Tweede Oosterparkstr.
Beukenw.
EIKENPL.
Derde Oosterparkstr.
C
D

Shopping Practicalities

Opening hours

In general, shops are open between 1-6pm on Mondays and 9/10am-6pm Tuesday to Friday. Most have late-night shopping on Thursdays till 9pm, but close earlier on Saturdays, at 5pm. Some branches of the food retail chain Albert Heijn stay open until 8 or 10pm.

Where to shop on Sundays

You'll find shops open on Sundays in the city centre, on Kalverstraat, Damrak, Leidsestraat, and near the Noorderkerk, particularly in Herenstraat. The current trend more or less all across the city is for shops to open from around 12/1-5pm on the first Sunday of the month during the summer season. This is also true of the commercial district around the Rijksmuseum (with antique shops on Nieuwe Spiegelstraat and Van Baerle and P.C. Hooft street). The big stores (De Bonneterie, Vroom & Dreesmann, Bijenkorf, Hema, etc.) are also open on Sunday afternoons. Lastly, remember that several markets are held on Sundays, including the ones specialising in contemporary art, bric-a-brac and secondhand goods, antiques and flowers (the flower market is only open in summer, though).

Paying for your goods

Only buy from prosperous and respectable-looking dealers and beware of anything that seems like too much of a bargain. If you're buying a work of art, you can ask for a certificate of authenticity, which the seller is obliged to provide. Generally speaking, you must ensure that you get a receipt for all your purchases.

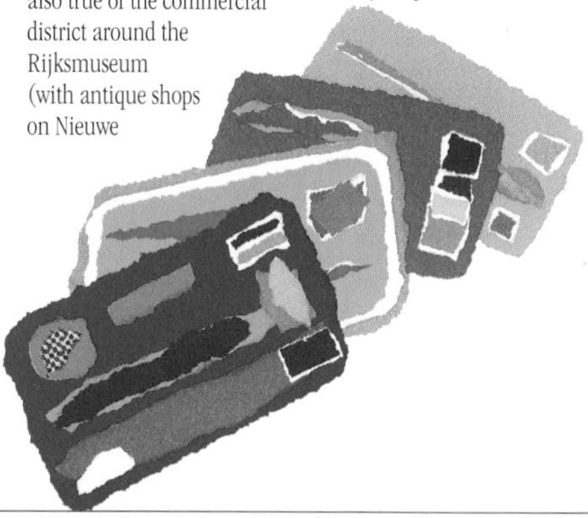

You may be asked to present it at customs and it may be useful should you ever want to resell an item, or when completing your insurance claim if you suffer a burglary.

Most shops will accept payment by card, especially Visa, Mastercard and Eurocard, for purchases over €22 or so. For other cards, you should check the stickers on the shop door before you go inside. Eurocheques and traveller's cheques are accepted everywhere.

How much you should pay

Traders are obliged by law to indicate the price of each item, so you won't get any nasty (or nice) surprises at the cash desk: there are labels everywhere. The only traders exempt from this requirement are dealers in secondhand goods and antiques, so you can usually indulge in a bit of haggling when buying from them. But remember, Holland has a long and proud history as a trading nation, so don't expect to get away with reductions of more than 10 or 15% on the original price.

Finding your way

Next to each address in the Shopping and Nightlife sections we have given its location on the map of Amsterdam on pages 82-83.

Customs formalities

There are no customs formalities for EU citizens when making purchases, provided you can show a receipt proving that duty on your purchase was paid in the Netherlands. There are no specific regulations in the case of antiques, as long as you can produce a certificate of authenticity and a bill made out by the seller.

International transportation

If you want to ship your new Malasian wood sofa home, or that pair of Delftware garden stools you've just treated yourself to, you have the choice of sending it by air, which is quick but expensive, or, if you are delivering it within Europe, by road, when how long it takes depends on how much you're prepared to pay. Insurance cover is almost always included in the transportation charge.

Here are a few useful addresses in Amsterdam:

Büch B.V.
☎ 696 37 77.
Specialist in the transportation of works of art by road and air. They deliver worldwide.

Hendriks B.V.
☎ 587 81 23.
Road transport of all types of goods. They deliver all over Europe.

Charter
☎ 654 32 10.
Air freight transport. They deliver worldwide.

If you're caught in possession of forged documents, the goods will be confiscated and you'll have to pay a heavy fine. You may also be charged with receiving stolen goods when you get back home.

Those who aren't resident in the European Union may be able to get a reimbursement of VAT paid on larger purchases, by means of a rather complicated procedure. If you want to do this, ask the seller for a special form (*certificaat van uitvoer* OB90), which you'll then have to fill in at the border.

For more information, contact the customs office at Schiphol airport: ☎ 316 47 00.

WOMEN'S FASHION

In the past women's fashion in the Netherlands has tended to be comfortable and well-made, in natural fibres, rather than outrageously fashionable. However in recent years independent designers have developed original styles, some wild, some smart, but often at very affordable prices for unique items, while the bright colours and artificial fabrics used in Dutch off-the-peg fashions will add zest to any young woman's wardrobe.

Fever

Prinsengracht, 194 (B1)
☎ 623 45 00
Westerkerk
Trams 13, 14, 17
Open Wed.-Fri. noon-6pm, Sat. noon-5pm.

Wilma Penning dresses elegant women who have a taste for adventure. Pride of place goes to silk and leather, with bright colours for every season. Here you'll find a light, transparent coat in pink silk, a smartly tailored jacket and matching accessories, such as hats and gloves. A peach of a collection.

Oilily

Van Baerlestraat, 26 (A3)
☎ 400 45 43
Open Tue.-Sat. 10am-6pm.

In this elegant, unfussy atmosphere, with lovely wood-panelling on the walls, you'll find young, exciting styles. Skirts, jumpers and blouson jackets in modern, brightly-coloured fabrics. This is the place to treat yourself to a pair of pink or yellow rubber boots to banish the grey from a rainy day. T-shirts between €36 and €64, trousers from €68.

Timeless Collection

Prinsenstraat, 26 (B1)
☎ 638 17 60
Noordermarkt
Open Mon.-Sat. 11am-6pm.

The shop's decor is as elegant as the clothes, in their sober tones and fine fabrics. The *Timeless* collection favours silks and natural fibres such as wool, cotton and suede, depending on the season. Here you'll find smart suits, simple evening dresses, swimsuits and a wide range of classic shirts and jackets. Nothing is very thrilling, but every item is well-designed, sensible, wearable and made in beautiful fabrics. A jacket will cost you around €180.

Qe Hoed van Tijn

Nieuwe Hoogstraat, 15 (B/C2)
☎ 623 27 59
Open Mon.-Sat. 11am-5pm.

Hats off to De Hoed van Tijn, a hat fanatic who has been collecting, designing and making hats for 25 years. He produces both classic hats, perfect for Ladies' Day at Ascot, and totally wild hats for his

theatrical and more flamboyant clients. He'll give you your own unique design, made-to-measure, in any style you like. Expect to pay around €90 to 180.

M/L Collections

Hartenstraat, 5 (B2)
☎ 620 12 16
Dam
Open Tue.-Fri. 11am-6pm, Sat. 10am-5pm.

The ultimate in Dutch off-the-peg fashions in a high-tech black and white decor. Here you'll find nothing that's too eccentric. Instead the clothes are elegant and lovely to wear, made using natural as well as synthetic fibres. Prices are reasonable and, if you come during the sales, you can get some really fantastic bargains. Jackets around €288, blouses €52, skirts €102 and trousers €136.

Henk Hendriks Couture

Herengracht, 360 (between Huidenst. and Leidsegracht, B2)
☎ 620 41 96
Open Tue.-Sat. 11am-5pm.

Designer Henk Hendriks opens his studio to women, and sometimes men, creating exclusive, made-to-measure clothes. Designs are made up first in cotton for a perfect fit, after which you'll have to wait two weeks for your unique item to be completed in the fabric and colour of your choice. Clothes can be sent anywhere in Europe. Expect to pay €1360 for a man's suit and about €910 for a lady's suit or a dress.

Demask

Zeedijk 64 (C1/2)
☎ 620 56 03
Centraal Station
Open Mon.-Sat. 10am-7pm, Thu. until 9pm, Sun. noon-5pm.

Surprise yourself and your partner by paying a visit to this highly specialised shop. *Demask* offers lingerie in lacquered leather, with chains and nails for the more extrovert. You can also find rubber mini-skirts, long latex gloves and some very saucy bodices. And in the back room you'll find enough unusual items to awaken the very demon within, even if you've got absolutely no imagination at all!

Hester van Eeghen

Hartenstraat, 37 (B2)
☎ 626 92 12
Dam
Open Tue.-Sat. 11am-6pm.

There's no two ways about it: if you want a truly original handbag, this is the place to come. Round, square or triangular, Hester Van Eeghen puts the fun back into functional. While the designs are Dutch, the gorgeous

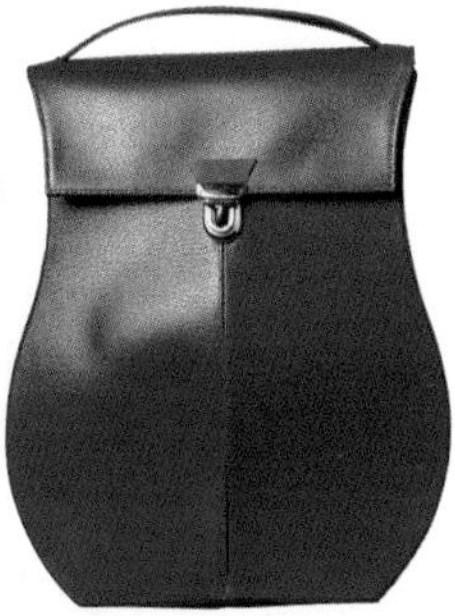

coloured leather is Italian, and what's more they're made in Italy too. To complete the look, buy a matching wallet, key-ring, credit card-holder and diary in the same leather and colour.

Cellarrich Connexion

Haarlemmerdijk, 98 (B1)
☎ 626 55 26
Open Mon. 1-6pm, Tue.-Fri. 10am-6pm, Sat. 10am-5pm.

It's the price of success – the four girls who started out selling leather goods in a cellar near Prinsengracht have had to move to a larger shop. They've kept the same minimalist decor, though, to show their creations off to best advantage. The bags and

accessories have an amusing touch, on which their reputation was originally based – real leather and fake crocodile skin, knitted leather pouches and trapezoid bags.

Vanilia

Van Baerlestraat, 30 (A3)
☎ 587 73 00
Trams 2, 3, 5, 12
Open Tue.-Sat. 10am-6pm, Thu. until 9pm, Mon. 1-6pm, Sun. noon-5pm.

Styles from the 1920s and 30s in colours and cuts to raise a few eyebrows. Lots of cotton, as well as fluid synthetic fabrics that are lovely to wear. The prices are pretty

affordable considering the shop's chic, expensive location. Trousers at €73, jackets at €100.

Hoeden M/V

Herengracht 422 (B2)
☎ 626 30 38
Leidsestraat
Trams 1, 2, 5, 11
Open Tue.-Sat. 11am-6pm, Thu. until 9pm.

The great drawing-room of this old residence provides the showcase for a wonderful collection of hats created by Dutch, German and British designers.

Here you'll find an enormous range, in every colour and material you can think of, from simple styles at €37 to sumptuous wide-brimmed straw hats at €363. On a practical note, the personal fitting service (reduction or enlargement) will give you the style you want in the size you want in under an hour.

Van Heek Lust for Leather

Lindengracht, 220 (A/B1)
☎ 627 07 78
Open Sat. noon-6pm and by appointment midweek.

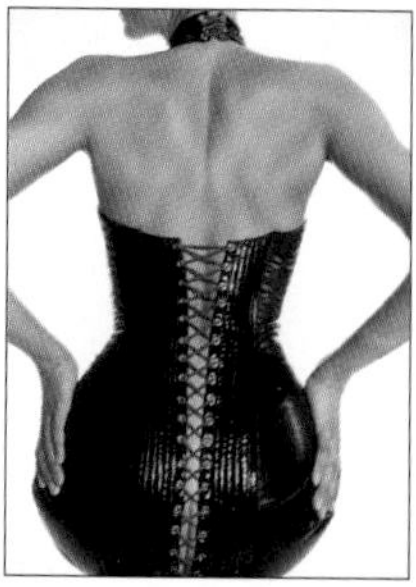

Joyce Van Heek both designs and makes her leather wear for men and women, including lingerie, waistcoats, trousers and skirts, some with daringly gaping laces at the back. There are many designs and sizes to choose from, but you can also have items made-to-measure. If you think you may want to use this service, have some information sent before you leave for Amsterdam. The use of very fine calfskin justifies the slightly higher prices (lace-up skirt around €180).

De Petsalon

Hazenstraat, 3 (A2)
☎ 624 73 85
Jordaan, Lauriergracht
Open Tue.-Sat. 11am-6pm.

In a city where the bicycle is king it hardly comes as a surprise that there's a shop specialising in helmets made in all kinds of

shapes and materials. For real class, you can't go much further than a matching helmet and saddle! This very kitsch shop also offers crazy belts and sunglasses to add the finishing touches to your ultra-cool look.

Female & Partners

Spuistraat, 100 (B1/2)
☎ 620 91 52
Open Tue.-Sat. 11am-6pm, Thu. until 9pm, Sun. and Mon. 1-6pm.

Amsterdam's top shop for erotic lingerie for women (and their partners) is not for the shy or faint-hearted. Esther and Ellen are pioneers in their field, offering an entire range of contemporary erotic fashions. The *Viva Maria, Undressed* and *Murray & Vern* collections are the best in the genre. The huge tattoo sported by the young woman behind the counter gives an indication of the kind of eccentricities you'll find inside.

Analik

Hartenstraat, 36 (B2)
☎ 422 05 61
Dam
Open Mon. 1-6pm, Tue.-Sat. 11am-6pm.

Young Dutch designer Analik has created a line of hip clothing and she's already had her own Paris show, in October 2000. The fabrics all have that feel-good factor, and the lines are distinctly modern and feminine, while practical enough for the busiest lifestyle.

Eva Damave

Tweede Laurierdwarsstraat, 51c (A2)
☎ 627 73 25
Jordaan
Trams 13, 14, 17
Open Wed.-Sat. noon-6pm.

With extravagant little jumpers, woollen skirts and jackets, extraordinary colours and original designs, Eva is the queen of knitwear. More sophisticated shoppers will particularly like the wonderfully comfortable jumpers embroidered in silk. Spoil yourself, they're not that expensive (around €70-90 for a jumper).

Clothes and Shoe Sizes

Don't forget that on the continent shoe sizes and clothes sizes may differ from what you are used to, but the sales assistant should be able to help you find the perfect fit. To help you navigate your way through the different sizes and choices we have included conversion tables on page 126. These list not only clothes and shoe sizes, but also weights and measurements.

MEN'S FASHION

For a long time now elegant Dutch men have been sporting Italian fashions, which are well represented in the chic shops of Van Baerlestraat and P.C. Hooftstraat. Dutch men's fashions aren't terribly inventive, with two exceptions – sportswear, which is well-made, practical and reasonably cheap, and the impeccably-cut leather wear.

Robin & Rik

Runstraat, 30 (A/B2)
☎ 627 89 24
Spui, Trams 1, 2, 5
Open Mon. 2-6pm, Tue.-Sat. 11am-6pm.

All you need to dress in leather from head to toe – trousers, jackets, tops, waistcoats and caps in different leathers and skins. Those who like close-fitting clothes should note that Robin and Rik also make made-to-measure garments. Nothing you could really wear to a business meeting, but guaranteed to cause a stir at the nearest gay club.

The Shirt Shop

Reguliersdwarstraat, 64 (B2)
☎ 423 20 88
Open every day 1-7pm.

If you're after a classic shirt, don't bother looking in this little shop. Here they're made of satin, velvet or moiré silk, or patterned with spots or checks. In other words – shirts for going out clubbing, trying out your chat-up lines, or just strutting your stuff. The brands are British, Dutch and sometimes Italian, all very exclusive and trendy. If you feel daring you could try the patchwork shirt (€89), or the Elvis T-shirt, fit for a king!

Thomas Grogg

Prinsenstraat, 12 (B1)
☎ 320 16 58
Open Mon. 1-6pm, Tue.-Fri. 11am-6pm, Sat. 11am-5pm.

The only boutique in the Netherlands selling clothing from Sweden. The five names on the sign indicate young, laid-back, elegant fashions: jeans, T-shirts and shirts, or more classic jackets in leather and linen. There's definitely something here for everyone.

Dockers

Leidsestraat, 11 (B2/3)
☎ 638 72 92
Trams 1, 2, 5, 11
Open Tue.-Sat. 9.30am-6pm, Thu. until 9pm, Mon., Sun. noon-6pm.

Levi's famous line of casual trousers, shirts, polo shirts and jackets, in a wide range of colours and cuts, which maintain the

comfort and quality on which the world-wide reputation of the brand is based. The usual range of American sizes.

Haberdashery

P.C. Hooftstraat, 53 (off map)
☎ 672 01 89
Trams 2, 3, 5, 12
Open Tue.-Fri. 10am-6pm, Thu. until 9pm, Sat. 10am-5pm, Sun. 1-5pm, Mon. 1-6pm.

This shop specialises in made-to-measure suits for businessmen who lack imagination and is the only place in the Netherlands to sell this particular German brand. If you want to be practical, you can have a second pair of trousers made to match the jacket, while those with long arms or large necks can have their shirts altered accordingly. Anything is possible here and the prices aren't too wild (€227-363 for a suit). Quality guaranteed.

Hoeden M/V

Herengracht, 422 (B2)
☎ 626 30 38
Leidsest. Trams 1, 2, 5, 11
Open Tue.-Sat. 11am-6pm, Thu. until 9pm.

If you're looking for a real panama hat or a Borsalino, or perhaps a cap or a boater, then hurry along to Marly Vroemen's shop, which specialises in hats for both men and women. A Borsalino will set you back about €90 and it will be altered to fit your head in the twinkling of an eye.

Sissy-Boy

Van Baerlestraat, 12 (A3)
☎ 672 02 47
Kalverstraat, 199 (B2)
☎ 638 93 05
Open Tue.-Sat. 9.30am-6pm, Thu. until 9pm, Mon., Sun. noon-6pm.

Don't be put off by the name, this excellent Dutch label creates sporty, contemporary clothes aimed at 20-30 year-olds. The cuts tend to be fairly conventional, but they're not afraid to use colour here, and you can find some more amusing styles. The prices are in everyone's range: shirts at €45, trousers €68-90.

Continental sizes

Men's shoe sizes are also different on the continent and clothes generally tend to be cut on the generous side. See the conversion tables on page 126 for more information.

Adrian

Prinsengracht, 130A (B1)
☎ 639 03 20
Open Tue.-Sat. noon-6pm.

If you dream of finding a really elegant, original shirt, then Adrian's your man. His shirts come in fabrics of every hue, to suit both conservative and eccentric tastes, and they're chosen in Italy and tailored in London. All that's left for you to do is to match them with jackets and shoes selected with care by the designer himself .

FOR CHILDREN

In Amsterdam, they did away with traditional layettes years ago. Here the by-word is imagination, with natural fibres, comfortable clothes and matching accessories. Classic, sporty, colourful or ultra-cool, your only problem is you're spoilt for choice. To make your children's happiness really complete, why not take them to a toyshop as well?

Trix & Rees

Sint Antoniesbreestrat, 130 (C2)
☎ 420 25 30
Metro Nieuwmarkt
Open Tue.-Sat. 10am-6pm, Mon. 1-6pm, Sun. noon-5pm.

Why shouldn't children be trendy too? Sheepskin jackets, chunky wool jumpers and T-shirts in natural cotton. Of course, everything is cut primarily for comfort, and the clothes are quite roomy. Modern mums will find everything for children aged 0-8 here, as well as 'adult' versions for themselves. Be prepared to pay €45 for a T-shirt and €59 for a little dress.

Oilily Store

P.C. Hooftstraat, 131-133 (off map)
☎ 672 33 61
Trams 2, 3, 5, 12 .
Open Mon. 1-6pm, Tue.-Fri. 10am-6pm, Thu. to 9pm, Sat., Sun. 10am-7pm.

If you've had enough of powder blue and pastel pink, Oilily has a line of bright, imaginative, colourful clothes, adorned with little flowers, hearts, butterflies and checks. They also have a matching range of accessories such as bags, shoes, socks, wooden jewellery and hair clips. Of course, you have to pay for style (embroidered T-shirt from €36-55, ensemble around €90).

De Beestenwinkel!

Staalstraat, 11 (C2)
☎ 623 18 05
www.beestenwinkel.nl
Open Tue.-Fri. 10am-6pm, Sat. 10am-5pm, Sun. noon-5pm.

This extraordinary shop on the corner of the street is an Aladdin's cave of toys: wooden toys, puppets, and heaps of gorgeous soft toys with realistic, expressive faces that parents will fall in love with and children will long to cuddle. This is the perfect place to come if you need a gift for a new baby.

't Klompenhuisje

Nieuwe Hoogstraat, 9A (B/C2)
☎ 622 81 00
Metro Nieuwmarkt
Open Mon.-Sat. 10am-6pm.

A prettily-decorated shop which is a real paradise for children's footwear. The company started out as a specialist producer of children's clogs, but has since expanded its production to other kinds of shoes, including sandals, walking boots and smart shoes. Expect to pay around €14 for a pair of clogs and €45 for a more complicated type of shoe.

Teuntje

Haarlemmerdijk, 132 (B1)
Jordaan
☎ 625 34 32
Open Mon. 1-6pm, Tue.-Fri. 10am-6pm, Sat. 10am-5pm.

Here they stock Danish, Belgian and Dutch brands that you can't find elsewhere, with clothes in cotton and other comfortable fabrics. Browns, dark greens and black are the common shades of this well-cut, practical clothing, sold at good prices (from €5.50).

De Speelmuis

Elandsgracht, 58 (A2)
☎ 638 53 42
Open Mon. 1-6pm, Tue.-Fri. 10am-6pm, Sat. 10am-5pm.

Children's clothes sizes

As with adult clothes, the cut of Dutch children's clothes tends to be quite generous.
0-1 year: 56/74cm (22/29in);
1-3 years: 80/98cm (32/39in);
3-8 years: 104/176cm (40/69in).

Who could resist these exquisite dolls' houses, filled of charming details that will take you back to your childhood? You're suddenly transported to Lilliput, in a fairy-tale world filled with miniature sofas, vases, flowers and tables, where adults just seem too big! Some of the more fragile, expensive items are really the preserve of specialist dolls' house collectors rather than children. House prices start at €45. They also stock a fine range of wooden toys and spinning tops. It's a paradise for the young and the young at heart.

De Kinderbrillenwinkel

Nieuwezijds Voorburgwal, 129 (B2)
☎ 626 40 91
Open Tue.-Fri. 11am-6pm, Sat. 11am-5pm.

This amazing shop specialises in spectacles for children. Here you'll find frames to suit every taste – green, yellow or blue, round or oval and always unusual and different. If your children are unpersuadably vain, and you happen to have their prescription handy, you can even buy safe, comfortable contact lenses specially adapted for their eyes. There's also a wide range of amusing old frames available from around €68 a pair. And don't forget, you can easily have the correct lenses fitted when you get home.

Belltree

Spiegelgracht, 10 (B3)
☎ 625 88 30
Rijksmuseum
Trams 6, 7, 10
Open Tue.-Sat. 10am-6pm, Mon. 1-6pm.

Here you'll find wonderful dolls' tea-sets with Delftware decorations, amazing musical boxes, kaleidoscopes, mechanical toys and roundabouts, not to mention educational toys to teach your children all about the planet they inhabit; in other words, wonderful toys for children of all ages (from €1.50).

FLOWERS AND GARDENS

Amsterdammers are true worshippers of flowers and plants, which they use to decorate their homes, balconies and gardens. It's hard not to be caught up by this passion when you walk past the stalls in the flower market, particularly since the prices are so low and there's such a wealth of choice, especially for plants grown from bulbs.The garden furniture and earthenware pots are also very tempting.

Riviera

Herenstraat, 2-6 (B1)
☎ 622 76 75
Noordermarkt
Open Tue.-Fri. 9am-6pm, Sat. 9am-5pm, Sun. noon-5pm.

Here you'll find loads of ideas for decorating your garden, as well as the prettiest floral arrangements in town. Lights with reflectors, wrought-iron lamps (€23), scented candles, cane armchairs, bronze bowls and teak garden furniture, not to mention engraved crystal glasses. If you really can't resist a superb teak bench (€204-545) or lounger (€272), they can be sent back home for you. The best place in Amsterdam for all garden-lovers.

Vivaria

Ceintuurbaan, 5 (off map)
☎ 676 46 06
Open Tue.-Fri. 10am-6pm, Sat. to 4pm.

This amazing shop sells nothing but terrariums, little indoor greenhouses in which you can easily grow ferns, lichens, mosses and wild orchids that resemble the primeval forest where all life began. These tiny decorative gardens are housed inside panes of glass set into frames of different shapes and sizes and more or less look after themselves, as long as you make sure they have water and light. It's like having an aquarium without fish, just as decorative, but much less hassle.

De Zon

Reestraat, 1 (A2)
☎ 627 22 13
Open Mon.-Sat. 9am-6pm.

Under a sumptuous canopy of purple fabric, flowers and plants take centre stage in a baroque composition that is pure theatre. *De Zon* sells flowers singly, and it's down to Johan, Mirjam and Masja to arrange them in a natural explosion of colour and fragrance – pure poetry. Be assured, you won't have seen a florist like this before!

Outras Coisas

Herenstraat, 31 (B1)
☎ 625 72 81
Noordermarkt
Open Mon. noon-6.30pm, Tue.-Fri. 10am-6.30pm, Sat. 5.30pm.

Crockery and garden furniture that's so beautiful and simple you'd be happy to use it inside as

well. Pretty cotton tablecloths, enamelled dishes with matching napkins, stoneware crockery, picnic hampers and large candles in unusual shapes. The lovely Dutch-made ironwork tables are around €125 each. Lots of decorative ideas for your patio or balcony, and for your living-room as well.

Growing Dutch bulbs

Bulbs for planting are sold from June to the end of December. If the winter has been hard, bulbs won't be available before the end of June at the earliest. Bulbs planted in the autumn will flower in spring, whereas those planted in spring (such as begonias, lilies and dahlias) will flower in autumn. If you have a heavy, clay soil, lighten it with sand and peat. (See also p.19 on growing tulips.)

Flower Market

Amstelveld (C3)
Prinsengracht
Tram 4.

Less well-known than the floating market of Singel, this charming flower market is held on Monday mornings on the shady Amstelveld square, near a wooden church. Stalls stacked with cut flowers rub shoulders with others selling indoor or garden plants.

Kees Bevaart

Singel (opposite 508, B2)
☎ 625 82 82
Muntplein
Trams 4, 9, 14, 16, 24, 25
Open every day 9.30am-5.30pm.

Of all the stalls in the floating market, this is the best stocked with hardy and seasonal plants. Here you'll find plant varieties you may never have seen before, as well as good advice on how to grow them.

De Tuin

Singel (opposite 500, B2)
☎ 625 45 71
Muntplein
Trams 4, 9, 14, 16, 24, 25
Open Mon.-Sat. 8am-5pm, Sun. 9am-4pm.

This is *the* place to buy tulips, with a very extensive range, including the famous black tulip *Queen of Night*. There are also 500 different species of bulbs, such as narcissus, daffodils, dahlias, hyacinths, lilies, freesias, begonias and amaryllis. Those not well versed in bulb cultivation can have everything explained to them in English (around €3 for ten tulip bulbs).

Entresol

Kloveniersburgwal, 135A (B/C2)
☎ 620 61 65
Open Mon.-Fri. 9am-6pm, Sat. 9am-2pm.

Entresol use different shades of green in their bouquets, which has the effect of drawing the eye to the few carefully-chosen touches of colour from the sumptuous flowers. As a result, the arrangements have a natural, wild quality that belies the subtle artistry behind them.

JEWELLERY AND ETHNIC GOODS

As well as the diamond trade, solidly established in Amsterdam since the 17th century, there are a number of shops and galleries specialising in ethnic goods. From magnificent jewellery in silver and coral, to masks from Africa and the Pacific and traditional earthenware crockery, each item reflects a different culture or part of the world.

Hans Appenzeller

Grimburgwal, 1 (B2)
☎ 626 82 18
Open Tue.-Sat. 11am-5.30pm.

For 30 years Hans Appenzeller has created refined, contemporary jewellery, taking his inspiration both from nature and the industrial world. His rings resemble unfurling flower stems, or evoke

the undulating contours of an orchid, with a pearl nestling at its heart. His necklaces, on the other hand, appear to have been fashioned from pieces of linking metal that have grown together of their own accord.

Beaufort

Grimburgwal, 11 (B2)
☎ 625 91 31
Open Tue.-Fri. 11am-6pm, Sat. 11am-5pm.

The jewellery collection on sale here is designed and produced by two young women, who work mostly with gold and silver, often producing pieces that contrast the two metals. The simple geometric lines are enhanced by an occasional pearl or diamond, in a harmonious marriage of classic and modern design.

Aboriginal Art

Prinsengracht, 570 (A2/B3)
☎ 422 22 12
Open Tue.-Sat. 11am-5.50pm.

The rich, highly contemporary works on show here can at first glance be mistaken for abstract art. They are in fact references to aboriginal paintings that depict the creation of the world by mythical ancestors. The *digeridoos*, musical instruments made from eucalyptus branches hollowed out by termites, as well as the paintings on canvas and bark, evoke an art form almost as old as time itself.

Kashba

Staalstraat, 3 (C2)
☎ 623 55 64
Muntplein
Open Mon.-Sat. 11am-6pm, Sun. 1-5pm.

KASHBA

This pretty shop contains the finds gathered on the course of the journeys of an indefatigable traveller who spends his time wandering the steppes of central Asia and the Indian subcontinent. Here you'll find furniture from Rajasthan and southern India, including carved doors and lintels, as well as *ikate* cloth and items of jewellery combining silver, turquoise, coral and lapis-lazuli. The high quality of these objects is reflected in the prices.

Gallery Steimer

Reestraat, 25 (A2)
☎ 624 42 20
Dam
Open Tue.-Fri. 11am-6pm, Sat. 11am-5pm.

This artisan jewellery-maker creates classic, timeless pieces full of invention. He draws the majority of his ideas from the past. If you'd like to wear jewels like those worn by queen Nefertiti or a bracelet to make you feel like a Celtic princess or Roman goddess, then Klaus Steimer will fulfil all your dreams. By cleverly combining gold, silver and semi-precious stones, he produces jewellery in antique styles, which he interprets with imagination to give them a contemporary feel. You can also have the piece of your choice made to order.

Bonebakker & Zoon

Rokin, 88-90 (B2)
☎ 623 22 94
Trams 4, 9, 14, 16, 24, 25
Open Mon.-Fri. 10am-5.30pm, Sun. noon-4pm.

This jeweller has supplied beautiful items to kings and princes since 1792, and all his products are strictly top of the range. It's worth having a look at the window display, though, even if you haven't the slightest intention of splashing out on anything. Although the diamonds are no longer cut on the premises, they're mounted in superb settings, as are other precious stones. Certificates are provided for all items (the gold is 18 carats). The service and quality are worthy of royalty – with prices to match.

De Rare Kiek

Prinsengracht, 539 (A2/B3)
☎ 620 98 60
Open Fri.-Sat. 1-6pm, or by appt.

This is the lair of a real character who has spent much of his life in Africa and drinks *jenever* like water. His name is Ger, and he has hundreds of fetishes, masks, statuettes and jewellery from all over Africa and the Pacific in an old warehouse full of interesting nooks and crannies. Collectors and museum curators have begun to take an interest, so go and see them before it's too late.

Jewellery Tips

In Holland every piece of gold or silver jewellery is stamped with an authenticating mark awarded by Gouda. This varies according to the number of carats (for 18 carat gold it's a tulip). In the case of ethnic jewellery on the other hand, there are no marks guaranteeing silver content or the authenticity of amber. A word of advice: amber is very rare and expensive. It has electrostatic qualities and gives off a slight scent when rubbed, for example, if the beads in a necklace are rubbed against each other.

SOMETHING A LITTLE DIFFERENT

In this city that's so like a village, you have to make an effort to stand out from your neighbours. Recent times have seen the opening of a great many unusual shops specialising in surprising and sometimes downright bizarre goods. Most of these are in Jordaan and beyond Prinsengracht. Now you have the chance to explore them.

Christmas Palace

Singel, 508-510 (B2)
☎ 421 01 55
Open Mon.-Sat. 9am-6pm, Sun. 10am-6pm.

Beat the last-minute rush by calmly choosing your Christmas decorations here. Angels, garlands, gilded candles, paper napkins decorated with stars, Christmas trees, Father Christmases and even a special edition of Delftware for your Christmas dinner table, in other words everything you need to prepare for the festive season to the sound of carols and Christmas songs, all year round.

Maranon

Singel, 488-490 (A/B2)
☎ 622 59 38
Trams 4, 9, 14, 16, 24, 25
Open Mon.-Sat. 9am-6pm, Sun. 10am-5pm.

With a range of 150 hammocks from South America, there's no way you could fail to find one you'd just love to hang out in. Indoor hammocks in cotton and sisal, outdoor hammocks in hemp, in varying sizes, from 3m/4ft to 6m/8ft, and various weights, from light to heavy canvas, for one or two people. Prices range from around €36 for a net hammock to €97 for a hand-embroidered one.

Tangam

Herenstraat, 9 (B1)
☎ 624 42 86
Open Mon. 1-6pm, Tue.-Sat. 11am-6pm, Sun. by appt.

This is a great place to stock up on lots of small gifts that won't break the bank (average price around €2.25). Check out the lamps, truly original creations that look like luminous shell garlands, or maybe the unique lightbulbs, decorated in silicon with coloured glass balls inside. Guaranteed to give your home a very special glow.

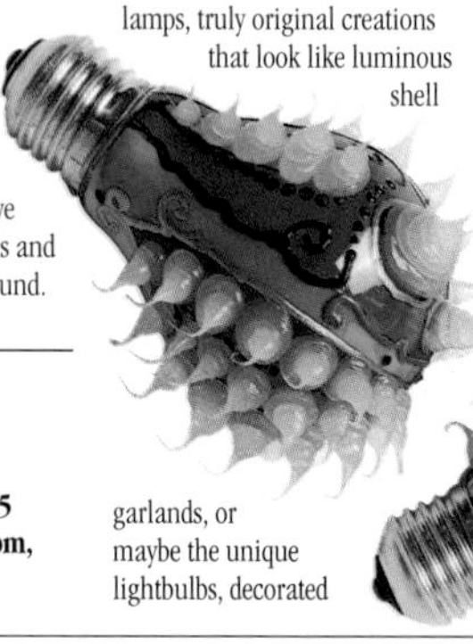

Knopenwinkel

Wolvenstraat, 14 (A/B2)
☎ 624 04 79
Spui
Trams 1, 2, 5
Open Tue.-Fri 11am-6pm, Sat. 11am-5pm.

The walls of this shop are literally covered with buttons. You can't fail to find the one you need or one to inspire your dressmaking. For 10 years Dorothea de Boer has been collecting thousands of buttons of all shapes, colours and

sizes. You'll find over 8,000 different buttons here, which should give even the least imaginative dress-maker some ideas.

De Witte Tandenwinkel

Runstraat, 5 (A3)
☎ 623 34 43
Open Mon. 1-6pm, Tue-Fri. 10am-6pm, Sat. 10am-5pm

A colourful treat for your teeth! This is the toothbrush palace. Fluorescent, Mickey Mouse-shaped, electric, designer – you'll find them all here, along with the most sophisticated toothpaste and most amazing tooth mugs. Everything to liven up your daily brushing routine and great ideas for amusing, inexpensive little gifts.

't Mannetje in Transport

Frans Halsstraat, 26A (B3)
☎ 679 21 39
www.manbike.nl
Open Tue.-Fri. 9am-6pm, Sat. 9.30am-5pm.

Don't leave Amsterdam without at least considering purchasing a bicycle. This is a shop that all pedal-pushing enthusiasts will love, with a wide range of unusual and made-to-measure bikes, adapted to suit all your needs. How about a real Dutch bike with back pedal brakes, or a tandem for inseparable lovers? Or why not invest in a rickshaw for doing your shopping, or carrying around a brood of happy children? You could go home with something unique that will make your friends envious.

Fun Frames

Tweede Egelantiersstraat, 14 (B1)
☎ 639 39 02
Jordaan, Westerkerk
Open Tue.-Fri. 11am-6pm, Sat. 10am-5pm.

This tiny shop specialising in ornate and unusual frames has recently opened in the heart of Jordaan. From smallest (2x3cm/¾x1in) to largest (20x30cm/8x12in), the plainest to the wildest, you can't accuse the frame designers from Holland and elsewhere of lacking imagination. Frames made from driftwood, hand-painted wood, metal, decorated with angels or shells, from €2.25-90 each.

Lush

Kalverstraat, 98 (B2)
☎ 330 63 76
Open Tue.-Fri. 9.30am-6pm, Thu. to 9pm, Mon. noon-6pm, Sun. 11.30am-6pm.

DON'T MISS:

Condomerie Het Gulden Vlies
Warmoesstraat, 141.
☎ 627 41 74 (see p. 49).
For every kind of condom.

Coppenhagen, 1001 kralen
Rozengracht, 54.
☎ 624 36 81 (see p. 53).
Hundreds of glass beads for you to make your own jewellery.

Fans of Lush from the UK will know that, despite appearances, nothing on display in this shop is actually edible. The long multicoloured cakes are actually made from soap, deodorant or solid shampoo, created from amazing fresh natural ingredients, such as the coffee bubble bath. Best of all is the self-service 'salad bar' with its dishes of body, face and foot cream. Just help yourself – with a spoon!

Interior Design

Gerrit Rietveld, one of the major exponents of the *de Stijl* movement, came to fame with his zig-zag chair, which could be easily mass-produced. Today's Dutch designers are just as creative, producing imaginative designs for furniture and lighting. Japanese furniture and exotic accessories match their strict, simple shapes to perfection.

Decor

Prinsengracht, 12 (B1)
☎ 639 24 42
Open Sat. 11am-5pm, sometimes open on Mon.

Decor is best known for its range of sofas which contrast baroque lines with contemporary black and white striped fabrics. Early 20th century antiques and curios, such as the metal latticework lockers, are merely there to set the scene, but they'll give you up-to-the-minute ideas for decorating your home at affordable prices.

Pakhuis Amsterdam

Oostelijke Handelskade, 17 (C1/2)
☎ 421 10 33
Open Mon.-Sat. 10am-5pm and some Sundays.

Housed in a former 19th century dockside warehouse, Pakhuis Amsterdam has 7,000 sq m/ 75,000 sq ft entirely devoted to European design. Here you'll find all the very latest trends, with textiles on the ground floor, furniture and lighting on the first floor, and the latest designs from all the biggest names on the second. With everything on display you can come here to get inspiration, make comparisons or place orders, but you can't buy, as it's wholesale only.

The Frozen Fountain

Prinsengracht, 629 (A2)
☎ 622 93 75
Open Tue.-Fri. 10am-6pm, Mon. 1-6pm, Sat. 10am-5pm.

A new exhibition is held every month in this gallery-shop, showcasing the latest creations by talented young Dutch designers. From decorative items to made-to-measure furniture, you'll always find plenty of ideas and often ideal gifts to take home. Prices vary greatly, from €4.50 to €540. A hairdresser and stylist recently moved in, so you can make practical use of your time while you contemplate all these beautiful objects. A superb shop that absolutely should not be missed.

Koot

Raadhuisstraat, 55 (B2)
☎ 626 48 30
Trams 13, 14, 17
Open Mon. 1-6pm, Tue.-Fri. 9am-6pm Thu. until 9pm, Sat. 10am-5pm.

The new art of living Dutch-style, interpreted in lamps and objects created by great designers, including the fashionable Jan Des Bouvrie, Rob Eekhardt, Maroeska Metz and Anet van Egmond.

Gingillo Gallery

Herengracht, 300 (B2)
☎ 620 59 95
Open Mon. 1-4.30pm, Tue.-Fri. 10am-6pm, Sat. 11am-5.30pm.
Leidsestraat, 12 (B2/3)
Open Mon. noon-7pm, Tue.-Sat. 11am-7pm, Thu. to 9pm, Sun. noon-6pm.

Designer gift store par excellence. All the big names in European design are here – Zack, Alessi and a host of others. Lighter/pens, Davis watches, Ritzenhoff glasses and masses of kitchenware mostly in polished or brushed chrome. A cornucopia of original ideas.

Klamboe Unlimited

Prinsengracht, 232 (B2)
☎ 622 94 92
Jordaan, Lauriergracht
Open Tue.-Fri. 11am-6pm, special opening hours in winter.

In the heat of summer, what better than a stylish net draped around your bed to keep mosquitoes at bay? Here you'll find every imaginable kind of mosquito net or *klamboe*. They come on round or rectangular frames and are made of nylon, light cotton or polyester. Prices from €20 to €68 for large mosquito nets, €20 for a traveller's net.

Fanous Ramadan

Runstraat, 33 (A/B2)
☎ 423 23 50
Open Mon. 1-6pm, Tue.-Sat. 11am-6pm, Sun. 1-5.30pm.

A *fanous ramadan* is an Egyptian lamp which is lit on the very last evening of Ramadan. This little shop, on the corner of Runstraat and Prinsengracht, specialises in every kind of oriental lamp, including lamps made from glass, metal and copper. Here you'll find the rarest,

magical pieces to recreate the soft, mysterious light of the *Thousand-and-One Nights* in your own home.

Getting it home

If you can't resist an item of furniture that's just too cumbersome to take home with you, then try a local carrier or Danzas, who will deliver it in 1 to 4 days (see addresses p. 81). Standards for lighting are the same in Holland as in the UK. Items may need adapting for use in other countries.

De Ridder

Haartenstraat, 21 (B2)
☎ 623 11 80
Open Tue.-Sat. 9.30am-6pm.

De Ridder is a family business that was first established in this old house in 1896. Specialising in rattan furniture, attested by the original stained glass window, they have since branched out into cane and teak to create a range of quality, liveable furniture at reasonable prices, upholstered in a range of brightly coloured fabrics that complement the natural tones.

Exploring the Markets

The way to explore a city's character is through its markets. Among the stalls, from the environmentally-friendly to the more high-brow, you'll discover the true nature of Amsterdam. Best of all are the flower and flea markets, where you'll find everything has a very cosmopolitan atmosphere.

Flower Market

Singel (B2)
Open every day in summer, 8am-5.30pm, closed Sun. in winter.

There's no way you could miss this market, which is centrally located and colourful all year round.

Flea Market

Waterlooplein (C2)
Metro Waterlooplein
Open Mon.-Sat. 10am-5pm

Amsterdam's biggest flea market specialises in secondhand clothes. Depending on your imagination and dressmaking skills, you should be able dress yourself for

next to nothing. What's more, as any designer will tell you, the best ideas come from flea markets. You'll also find shoes, books, CDs and records, old post-cards and army surplus, as well as stalls selling Indonesian cloth and Indian jewellery, some of which is very beautiful and hard to find elsewhere. The same can't be said of the dealers and pickpockets, who you need to watch out for. There's more pleasant discoveries to be found at the *Waterloo Ware House* (see box p.103), near by.

Stamp Market (*Postzegelsmarkt*)

Nieuwezijds Voorburgwal (B2)
Spui
Open Wed. and Sat. 1-6pm.

A stamp and old coin market is held twice a week opposite the Amsterdams Historisch Museum. Philatelists and coin collectors are sure to find something of interest here, and business is conducted in a very professional atmosphere.

Secondhand Book Market

Oudemanhuispoort (B/C2)
Muntplein
Open Mon.-Sat. 11am-5pm.

In a delightfully picturesque 18th-century passage between Kloveniersburgwal and Oudezijds Voorburgwal, you'll find stalls selling books for collectors as well as old engravings. Take the time to explore. The Dutch are very good linguists and you'll find books in many languages, including plenty in English. You might also find original engravings or facsimile reproductions of 17th, 18th and 19th-century Amsterdam landscapes. All in all, lots of interesting souvenirs that won't be hard to carry home.

Art Market (*Kunstmarkt*)

Spui (B3)
Trams 1, 2, 5, 11
Open Sun. 9am-6pm, Mar.-early Dec.

You'll find good and bad in this market, where contemporary

artists regularly come to sell their work, including raku pottery, watercolours, sculpture and oil paintings. One excellent engraver, Wim van der Meij, sells originals from €30 each. Where paintings are concerned, it's all a matter of taste, but what you see here often compares very favourably with accredited galleries showing contemporary art.

Book Market *(Boekenmarkt)*

Spui (B3)
Trams 1, 2, 5, 11
Open Fri. 10am-6pm.

Poets read out their verses to a highly distinguished background accompaniment of notes played on a harp, while lovers of old books and collectors of rare ones rifle through the piles of old leather-bound volumes looking for special editions. A fascinating market, and one that's very typical of Amsterdam.

Bird and Farm Produce Market

Noordermarkt (B1)
Jordaan
Open Sat. 9am-5pm and Mon. morning.

A lovely market, where ordinary Amsterdammers come to shop. Among the stalls selling farm produce you're likely to find chicks and homing pigeons, as well as more exotic birds. – a great place to bring children for a quick natural history lesson! It's also very popular with the

inhabitants of Jordaan, who flock to the cafés in the square when they've finished doing their shopping.

Albert Cuypmarkt General Market

A. Cuypstraat (off map)
Trams 4, 16, 24, 25
Open Mon-Sat. 9am-5pm.

The busiest and most popular of the city's markets. A truly cosmopolitan crowd rub shoulders among the stalls selling fish, poultry, fruit and vegetables, spices, cheeses, cheap clothes, pots and pans and leather goods.

Bric-a-brac Market

Nieuwmarkt (C2)
Metro Nieuwmarkt
Open Sun. 10am-5pm

A very disparate collection of items, from household objects to worn-out books and furniture on the verge of collapse. In other words, the ideal place to go rummaging, if you like that kind of thing. There's loads of choice, but you wouldn't want to be in a hurry. There are a few new items to be had if you get there early, particularly silverware, ceramics and glass, though ultimately it's not that cheap.

Waterloo Ware House

Jodenbreestraat, 144 (C2)
Open Mon-Sat. 9am-5pm, Sun. 11am-5pm.

From unusual objects to old ice-skates, this warehouse contains a thousand treasures at bric-a-brac prices. There's something here from every corner of the world – you'll find great big jugs and masks from Africa, but you might equally well come across an old piece of Delftware or an oriental carpet that's not too threadbare.

TABLEWARE AND FABRICS

Rare, beautiful and amusing objects from all over the world, particularly Asia, and fabrics in brilliant colours, for simple – or sumptuous – decorations for your home and table. Amsterdam has many shops selling fabrics you won't find easily elsewhere, but for a few years now high-tech decoration has been all the rage in Jordaan's shops, which keep a close eye on new fashion trends.

Kitsch Kitchen

Eerste Bloemdwarsstraat, 21-23 (A2)
☎ 428 49 69
Open Mon.-Fri. 11am-5.30pm, Sat. 10am-5pm.
Kitsch Kitchen Kids: Rozengracht, 183 (A2)
☎ 622 82 61
Open Mon.-Sat. 10.30am-6pm.

There's no need to go all the way to Mexico for amusing, brightly-coloured, kitsch and very plastic household equipment, there's loads of it here. Fluorescent brooms, violet ladles, flowery waxed table-cloths and shopping bags, tequila glasses (€2.25), *papel picado* for the Mexican Day of the Dead and amulets of the Virgin Mary from Guadeloupe.

Binnenhuis

Huidenstraat, 3-5 (B2)
☎ 622 15 84
Spui
Trams 1, 2, 5
Open Mon. 1-6pm, Tue.-Fri. 10am-6pm, Sat. 11am-5pm

Simply the best! A pioneer among shops selling contemporary and high-tech decorative items, whose products and new lines regularly feature in Dutch home style magazines. Metal shelves that make waves across the walls, tulip-shaped wall-lamps and some really wild crockery, as well as beautiful sheets with old-fashioned embroidery (€318). It isn't cheap, of course, but why not come and have a look anyway?

What's Cooking

Reestraat, 16 (A2)
☎ 427 06 30
Open Tue.-Fri. noon-6pm, Sat. 11am-6pm.

Calculating your fabric

Dutch fabrics don't come in standard widths. If you're planning to buy some fabric for curtains or soft furnishings, measure up before you go. The shop assistant should be able to help you calculate the amount of fabric you require. McLennan's silks come in widths of 1m/39in to 1.15m/45in), so you'll need 0.5m/20in for a standard size cushion cover.

Specialising in culinary delights, the ground and upper ground floors are devoted to all things blue and green, while the basement is filled with red, orange and yellow items. So you can fill a bowl with dry goods and sauces all of one colour to make a fun, original gift.

Freud & Co Koogerei

Runstraat, 2 (A/B2)
☎ 624 54 07
Open Mon. 1-6pm, Tue., Wed., Fri. 11am-6pm, Thu. 11am-9pm, Sat. 11am-5pm.

Wood or stoneware pestle and mortar sets, rolling pins and every conceivable kind of whisk are just some of the items in the wide range offered here. From designer kitchenware to humble enamel pots, with their bright colours and shiny stainless steel, even the smallest utensils are a work of art, and will get you rushing into the kitchen, keen to cook up something special.

De Haan & Wagenmakers

Nieuwezijds Voorburgwal, 97-99 (B2)
☎ 620 25 25
www.dutchquilts.com
Open Tue.-Fri. 10am- 5pm.

An essential stop for lovers of patchwork. For 15 years De Haan & Wagenmakers have been producing their own collection of fabrics for patchwork, and you won't find them anywhere else. Besides a fair few books and magazines on the subject, you can get a do-it-yourself kit or buy something ready-made.

Mc Lennan's Puresilk

Hartenstraat, 22 (B2)
☎ 622 76 93
www.puresilk.nl
Open Mon. 1-6pm, Tue.-Fri. 10.30am- 6pm, Sat. 10.30am-5.30pm.

Step into the enticing world of the finest silks selected in the workshops of China, Thailand and Vietnam. You'll find them stretched across the walls or raised like colourful banners. Raw, smooth, goffered, brocaded, satiny, printed and plain, this is where the Dutch couturiers come to stock up

with crepe de Chine, shantung, taffeta and silk brocade. Expect to pay around €27 a metre/39in for lightweight crepe de Chine and €49 for a heavier example. Truly magnificent materials and colours.

Studio Bazar

Reguliersdwarsstraat, 60-62 (B2)
☎ 625 26 25
Muntplein
Open Mon. 1-6pm, Tue.-Fri. 10am-6pm, Thu until 9pm, Sat. 10am-5pm.

Despite the somewhat off-putting 'warehouse' layout of this shop, it's here you'll find the best lines in crockery, table linens and kitchen utensils with a real contemporary feel. Frosted plastic 'Screwpull' corkscrews in a range of ten different colours (around €27), Mickey Mouse kettles, flexible non-stick cake-moulds (€30-40), cactus-shaped fruit-squeezers and smart wicker picnic hampers: a real classic for Sundays in the country that will never go out of style!

ANTIQUES AND CERAMICS

All the collectors are familiar with Nieuwe Spiegelstraat, where you'll find Amsterdam's finest antique shops. Alongside the more prestigious dealers there are also less well-known places where real bargains can be found, particularly fine pieces of old and new Delftware, which you could never find elsewhere. Engraved or sculpted glass is also a popular part of the decor of traditional Dutch interiors.

Hogendoorn & Kaufman

Rokin, 124 (B2)
☎ 638 27 36
Trams 4, 9, 14, 16, 24, 25
Open Mon-Sat. 10am-6pm, Sun. noon-6pm.

The best address in town for buying modern Delft or Makkum ware. Pieces are selected in the two royal factories and are hand decorated by the best craftsmen. Everything from lovely Delft tiles 13x13 cm/5x5in to elegant tulip vases, but you have to be prepared to spend some money – €23 for a decorated tile, €136 for a vase. The shop will have it sent home for you.

Holland Gallery De Munt

Muntplein, 12 (B2)
☎ 623 22 71
Open Mon-Sat. 10am-6pm.

Make no mistake, this isn't a souvenir shop. On the contrary, it's a specialist outlet for fine Dutch faience. All the pieces sold here are signed, and all are made in one or other of the royal factories: *Porceleyne Fles*, Delft, *Tichelaar* and Makkum. Faience tiles from €25. A very wide choice.

Eduard Kramer

Nieuwe Spiegelstraat, 64 (B3)
☎ 623 08 32
Rijksmuseum
Trams 6, 7, 10
Open Mon.-Sat. 10am-6pm, Sun. 1-6pm.

In this antique shop, specialising in old Delft and Makkum pieces, you have to pick your way with cat-like caution among the unbelievable piles of faience porcelain, glass and earthenware pipes. Here you'll find the widest choice of glazed tiles – a little expensive if you want a complete makeover for your kitchen or bathroom, but there's nothing to stop you using one as a table mat.

GOING, GOING… GONE!

Sotheby's
De Boelelaan, 30 (B3)
☎ 550 22 00
Open Mon.-Fri. 9am-5pm.
To get an idea of antique prices, take a look round Sotheby's. This famous British firm of auctioneers also has a branch in Amsterdam. Here you'll find sales catalogues showing the prices various items reached at auction. If you want to attend one of the sales, all the items are put on display beforehand.

Peter Korf De Gidts

Nieuwe Spiegelstraat, 28 (B3)
☎ 625 26 25
Rijksmuseum
Trams 6, 7, 10
Open Tue.-Sun. 12.30-5.30pm.

In the 18th century it was usual to give the gift of an engraved glass as a fragile souvenir of a religious or other family celebration. Fairly rare today, they're decorated with coats of arms, maxims, figures and landscapes. One of these would make a lovely, and typically Dutch gift.

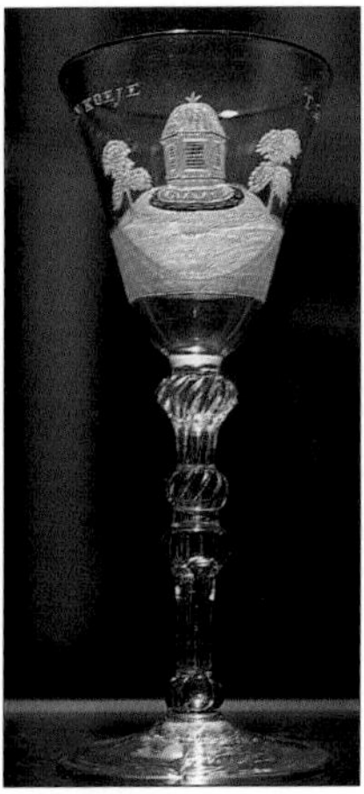

Toebosch

Nieuwe Spiegelstraat, 33-35 (B3)
☎ 625 27 32
Open Mon.-Fri. 11am-5.30pm, Sat. 11am-3pm

Amid the ticking of magnificent Dutch clocks, look out for the 18th century barometers and 19th century musical boxes, from tiny examples to huge, complicated feats of cabinet-making. The decor with its displays of sideboards, tables and chairs helps to recreate a typical Dutch interior.

Steenman & Van der Plas

Prinsengracht, 272 (B2)
☎ 627 21 97
Jordaan, Lauriergracht
Open Thu., Fri. 11am-6pm, Sat. 11am-5pm or by appt.

These pieces of office and shop furniture and accessories, designed from 1880-1920, are beautiful, simple and functional. A display of exceptional pieces, from large clocks to cabinets with sliding backs, all displayed in an attractive setting.

Ingeborg Ravestijn

Nieuwe Spiegelstraat, 57 (B3)
☎ 625 77 20
Open Mon.-Fri. 11am-6pm, Sat. 11am-5pm.

You'll find a selection of general antiques and plenty of silverware and ceramics in this shop. To give your table that original touch, you can buy replicas of Dutch glasses made in the Czech Republic. Prices range from around €20 for the smallest up to €32 for the larger ones with the long flutes.

Frides Laméris

Nieuwe Spiegelstraat, 55 (B3)
☎ 626 40 66
Open Tue.-Fri. 10am-6pm.

Antique faience and glassware from the 16th, 17th and 18th centuries, with drinking horns and pebble-bottomed glasses in the window, just like the ones you see in still life paintings by the Dutch old masters. Also a selection of Delftware and Chinese porcelain.

H.C. Van Vliet

Nieuwe Spiegelstraat, 74 (B3)
☎ 622 77 82
Rijksmuseum
Trams 6, 7, 10
Open every day 10am-6pm and by appt.

Continuing the tradition of Dutch master glassworkers, this antique shop is home to an extraordinary collection of 16th and 17th-century European glass. The selection of engraved glasses is particularly fine. They were originally given as gifts to mark a special occasion, such as a christening, wedding or birthday. There are many beautiful pieces of Italian or Flemish origin, as well as a large collection of period Dutch faience.

BRIC-A-BRAC

Bric-a-brac is something of a tradition in the Netherlands and is sold in all the city's markets. The real bargains are to be found in the antique shops, where prices may be a bit dearer but there's less doubt about authenticity. However, wherever you choose to shop, bargain-hunters are bound to unearth a few hidden treasures in the city, and for anyone mad about china, the Queen's Day bonanza is not to be missed!

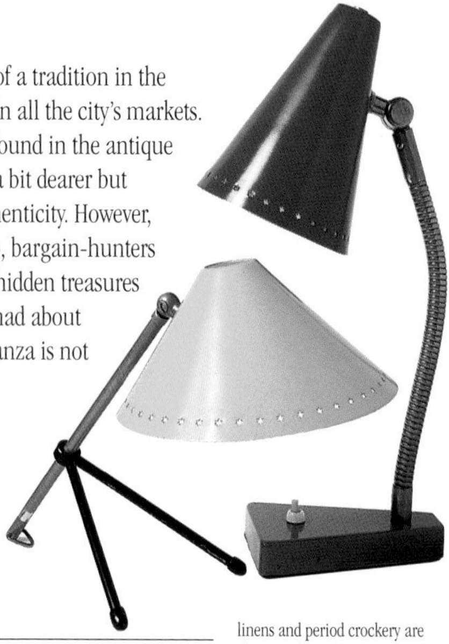

Fifties-Sixties

Huidenstraat, 13 (B2)
☎ 623 26 53
Spui
Trams 1, 2, 5, 11
Open Tue.-Sat. 1-6pm.

You'll find the owner of this shop, who personally guarantees the authenticity of her stock, surrounded by a charming jumble of lighting equipment and household electrical goods from the 1930s-60s. A fine selection of kitchen gadgets, crockery and lamps in absolutely unrepeatable designs, and they are not too expensive either. Not all of it would look right in just any home, but fans of 60s retro will be in seventh heaven. Expect to pay around €125 for a 1940s Philips lamp and €73 for a 1950s toaster.

& Klevering

Bloemgracht, 175-177 (A1/2)
☎ 422 03 97
Open Tue.-Fri. 11am-6pm.

A large warehouse selling period furniture and antiques such as cast-iron enamel baths and 1930s double washbasins in marble or stone. For the country kitchen look, they also stock simple cupboards in white leaded or polished wood, perfect for storing your crockery.

Puck

Nieuwe Hoogstraat, 1A (corner of Kloveniers-burgwal, C2)
Metro Nieuwmarkt
Open Mon.-Sat. 11am-6pm.

Lovers of retro clothes will find clothes here to wear at any time of day or night, such as lace nightgowns (€14), lingerie, laced bodices (€9), strappy evening dresses with sequins (€52), as well as period costume jewellery to match. Handmade, embroidered linens and period crockery are also on sale in this retro cornucopia.

Tut-Tut

Elandsgracht, 109 (De Looier antiekmarkt, A2)
☎ 627 79 60
Trams 7, 10
Open Wed.-Sat. 11am-5.30pm, Thu. to 9pm.

Among the antique-sellers in this little market is a stall specialising in old toys – dolls, robots, mechanical toys, and Fleischmann, Dinky and Matchbox trains (sometimes in the original box). Be prepared to haggle!

Conny Mol

Elandsgracht, 65 (A2)
☎ 623 25 36
Trams 7, 10
Open Wed.-Sat. 11am-5pm.

Conny Mol specialises in furniture, lighting equipment and objects dating from 1850 to 1945. In the large range, you'll find lovely Art Deco pieces such as lamps and wall lights in glass and chrome. Mirrors with wrought iron frames are also big news here.

Meulendijks & Schuil

Nieuwe Spiegelstraat 45A (B3)
☎ 620 03 00
Open Mon.-Sat. 10am-6pm.

An address to remember for all sailing fanatics and people interested in the history of the science of navigation, with old compasses, 18th-century sextants and chronometers. Loads of decorative and gift ideas, often less expensive than you'd expect.

Keystone Novelty Store

Huidenstraat, 28 (B2)
☎ 625 26 60
Spui
Trams 1, 2, 5, 11
Open Tue.-Sat. 11am-6pm.

Lovers of old toys will be amazed by the range in this shop, which also sells a selection of crockery and household electrical appliances from the 1950s. Dinky Toys at around €5 each, a Fleischmann locomotive for €175

and mechanical dolls for €37. Great prices for nostalgic grown-ups and plenty of choice for toy collectors.

Silverplate

Nes, 89 (B2)
☎ 624 83 39
Open Tue.-Sat. noon-6pm.

A stone's throw from *Rokin*, Kyra ten Kate has opened a shop selling 19th-century silverware and pieces in silver plate for a really elegant dinner table. A wide choice of both cutlery and dinner service items.

Nic Nic

Gasthuismolensteeg, 5 (B2)
☎ 622 85 23
Open Tue.-Fri. noon-6pm, Sat. 10am-6pm.

The owner of this shop is clearly doing just what she enjoys. The result is a stunning array of ironic bric-a-brac at reasonable prices,

De Rommelmarkt (Bric-a-brac Market)

Looiersgracht, 38 (A2)
Trams 7, 10
Open Sat.-Thu. 11am-5pm.

A few stalls indicate the entrance to this covered market on two floors, with two hundred permanent or temporary stands dealing in bric-a-brac. If you want to find that special bargain, your best chance is at the weekend.

ceramics, figures of patron saints, 60s and 70s lighting and candlesticks by Scandinavian designers for around €8.

TOBACCO, SPIRITS AND HERBAL REMEDIES

The Dutch are known for their love of good tobacco and their production (and consumption) of quality alcoholic drinks, so it's hardly surprising that Amsterdam has a great number of shops devoted to these forbidden fruits. You'll also find shops selling spices, full of scents reminiscent of hot and exotic Indonesia, reminders of Amsterdam's past, at the centre of a colonial empire.

P.G.C. Hajenius

Rokin, 92-96 (B2)
☎ 623 74 94
Between Dam and Muntplein
Open Mon. noon-6pm, Tue.-Sat. 9.30-6pm, Thu. until 9pm, Sun. noon-6pm

Even non-smokers should visit this smoker's paradise, where the superb Art Deco interior has remained unchanged since 1914. As soon as you step through the door, your nostrils are assailed by the mingled scents of tobacco. With its period wood-panelling and shelves filled with cigars, pipes and tobacco jars, *Hajenius* is a chic and classy shop, with a touch of old-fashioned stuffiness that's rather amusing, and has been renowned for 170 years for the subtle mix of flavours in its cigars, from cigarillos to coronas. You can also buy every kind of luxury accessory for smokers here – lighters, boxes, humidifiers, cigar cases and a colossal choice of earthenware, wooden and meerschaum pipes.

Herboristerie Jacob Hooy & Co

Kloveniersburgwal, 12 (B/C2)
☎ 624 30 41
Metro Nieuwmarkt
Open Mon. 10am-6pm, Tue.-Fri. 8.30am-6pm, Sat. 8.30am-5pm.

It's now the fifth generation of Oldenbooms who stand behind the antique counter of this shop, which has been in their family for a hundred and fifty years. They specialise in medicinal herbs and spices (with six hundred varieties), natural cosmetic products and sweets, including their famous licorice drops. Even if you decide not to buy anything, the shop itself is worth a visit just to see its shelves lined with jars.

The Natural Health Company 'De Munt'

Vijzelstraat, 1 (B3)
☎ 624 45 33
Muntplein
Open Mon.-Fri. 9.30am-6.30pm, Thu. until 9pm, Sat. 9.30am-6pm.

In this little shop vitamins and essential oils line the shelves, while bubble bath with plant extracts, or unusual soaps scented with cinnabar, orange or even cannabis, are sure to liven up bath time! All the products are completely natural, for glowing, healthy, baby-soft skin.

Van Coeverden

Leidsestraat, 58 (B2/3)
☎ 624 51 50
Trams 1, 2, 5, 11
Open Mon.-Sat. 10am-6pm.

A real old-fashioned tobacco shop, with a tiled floor and dark, wooden shelves filled with pipes, cigar boxes, packets of rolling tobacco and even cigarettes. The very walls themselves seem to be impregnated with the smell of tobacco. Nothing here seems to have changed much for decades and, even if you're not a smoker, it's worth stepping inside just to experience the atmosphere of one of these shops that are so typical of Amsterdam culture.

De Bierkoning

Paleisstraat, 125 (B2)
☎ 625 23 36
Dam
Open Mon. 1-7pm, Tue.-Fri. 11am-7pm, Thu. until 9pm, Sat. 11am-6pm, Sun. 1-5pm

However short your stay in Amsterdam, don't let it pass by without visiting a brasserie or other establishment for beer-drinking. This liquid has been flowing in Amsterdam's cafés since the 16th century. In *De Bierkoning* you'll find a selection of 850 different kinds of beer to take away. And for purists, there's even an appropriate glass to go with each type.

Oud Amsterdam

Nieuwendijk, 75 (B1/2)
☎ 624 45 81
Dam
Open Mon.-Sat. 10am-6pm.

In this very busy shopping street, *Oud Amsterdam* ('Old Amsterdam') is an old-fashioned shop with beams decorated with little bottles of spirits. Behind the counter, with its patina of age, you can see the fifty or so Dutch liqueurs on display, and particularly the seventeen types of *jenever* distilled here and aged for 1 to 17 years. Tasting essential.

Henri Bloem's

Gravenstraat, 8 (B2)
☎ 623 08 86
Dam
Open Mon. noon-6pm, Tue.-Fri. 10am-6pm, Thu. until 9pm, Sat. 10am-5.30pm.

This is more than just a shop selling spirits. Here you'll find someone who can really tell you all about the various *jenevers* and the subtle differences between *bessenjenever*, *oude jenever* and *korenwijn*. After that, you'll be able to buy with the confidence of a true connoisseur.

JENEVER OR BRANDY?

Jenever is flavoured with herbs and can be drunk young or old. It can also be distilled with lemon or redcurrants. Many people also enjoy the fruit brandies, such as *'Rose sans épines'* ('Rose without thorns'), made by monks, or *Oranje Bitter*, a syrupy orange liqueur which is drunk on 30 April, when the birthday of Queen Beatrix is celebrated.

COFFEE, TEA, CHOCOLATE AND SPICES

Would you like an *Amsterdammertje* or a *speculaasje* with your coffee? If you don't want to look like an ignoramus when faced with this kind of question, be sure to make an early visit to one of Amsterdam's excellent confectioners to sample the subtle flavours of bitter chocolate and ginger biscuits. Then savour the aroma of freshly-ground coffee emanating from one of the old cafés, most of which were founded at the time of the East India Company's first expeditions to the spice islands of the Far East. And if you'd like to try your hand at some Indonesian cooking, south Amsterdam is the place to go for the greatest range of exotic ingredients.

Geels & Co

Warmoesstraat, 67 (B2/C1)
☎ 624 06 83
Dam
Open Mon.-Sat 9.30am-6pm.

Founded 140 years ago, this family business in the heart of the red light district grinds 20 different types of coffee on the premises. A delicious aroma and a charming shop, where the boxes and jars look like something out of a 1930s film set. Worth a detour.

Simon Lévelt

Prinsengracht, 180 (B1)
☎ 624 08 23
Westerkerk
Open Mon. noon-6pm, Tue.-Fri. 9am-6pm, Sat. 9am-5pm.

Since 1839 this lovely shop decorated with wrought iron and situated opposite the Westerkerk has been selling 25 different sorts of coffee, all ground on the premises, and 100 special blends of tea. Not to be missed.

Wijs & Zonen

Warmoesstraat, 102 (B2/C1)
☎ 624 04 36
Dam
Open Mon.-Fri. 9am-5.30pm, Sat. 9.30am-5.30pm.

A pretty little shop with a lovely smell of coffee, which is stored in enamel jars. Generations have watched the repetition of the same ritual, when a taster comes to verify the standard of the forty different subtle blends of tea.

Puccini Bomboni

Staalstraat, 17 (C2)
☎ 626 54 74
Open Tue.-Sat. 10am-6pm, Sun. 1-6pm.

In this beautiful shop, where the light filters through stained-glass windows, exquisite chocolates are piled on the counter in precarious pyramids. Made by Ans van Soelen to old-fashioned recipes using butter and cocoa and no preservatives, they are truly delicious and certainly not for weight watchers!

The Trials and Tribulations of the Coffee Plant

The word 'coffee' comes from the name *Kaffa*, a region in Ethiopia where the coffee tree originates. When Arab merchants introduced the drink to Yemen, it became known as *Arabica* or *Moka*, the name of the port from which it was mostly exported. In 1714 Pancras, Mayor of Amsterdam, gave King Louis XIV of France a few coffee plants which the Dutch had acclimatised in their Indonesian colony of Batavia. The French then introduced them to Guyana and Brazil.

Toko Ramee

Ferdinand Bolstraat, 74 (B3)
☎ 662 20 25
Trams 16, 24, 25
Open Tue.-Fri. 9am-6pm, Sat. 9am-5pm.

Krupuk, ayam, sambal, gado gado, bami, nasi – you could play a guessing game, trying to match these Indonesian names to their products. On the other hand, if you want to buy with confidence, you'd be better off asking the advice of the charming Moluccan lady who sells the spices and can also explain to you how to use them to best advantage in your cooking. You can bring a real hint of adventure to your meals by concocting some true Indonesian dishes, and you can, of course, use these ingredients very successfully to spice up western-style food.

Arnold Cornélis

Elandsgracht, 78 (A3)
☎ 622 12 28
Jordaan
Trams 7, 10
Van Baerlestraat, 93 (off map)
☎ 662 12 28
Trams 3, 5, 12
Open Mon.-Fri. 8.30am-6pm, Sat. 8.30am-5pm.

In this renowned patisserie you'll find not only delicious fruit tarts *(Limburgse vlaai)*, but also confectionery, butter biscuits, *speculaas* – delicious with coffee – marzipan and chocolate, all homemade. The sweet-toothed Amsterdammer's favourite shop!

Australian Homemade

Leidsestraat, 59 (B2/3)
☎ 622 08 97
Singel, 437 (B2)
☎ 428 75 33
Open Mon.-Sat. 9am-6pm.

Chocoholics and art lovers alike will simply melt at the sight of these chocolates, all decorated with aboriginal designs. The picture of a kangaroo tells you it's a tea-flavoured centre, while tortoises indicate almond centres and the fish are ginger flavoured. Come and discover the other flavours for yourself, and don't miss the freshly-made ice cream.

Unlimited Delicious

Haarlemmerstraat, 122 (B1)
☎ 622 48 29
www.unlimiteddelicious.nl
Open Mon.-Fri. 9am-6pm, Sat. 9am-5pm.

There's nothing dull about these chocolates. White, dark or milk, the flavour of cocoa beans is subtly enhanced by balsamic vinegar, Espelette peppers,

red peppers and even tomatoes! There are some 25 different combinations, each one unusual and unique. Book up a month in advance and you can even learn how to make them for yourself, under the instruction, of course, of a master chocolate-maker.

SECONDHAND GOODS

The Dutch love a bargain. For secondhand clothes, try the markets on Waterlooplein and Noordermarkt, where the great revival of 1970s clothes is in full swing. If you prefer more of a classic look, it's better to go to the specialist shops in Jordaan. Many shops in Kalverstraat and Nieuwendijk have sales on all year round, and, like everywhere else, the smartest time to buy is when you see posters in the windows proclaiming *'Uitverkoop'* or *'Opruiming'*. Sales are held twice a year, starting in the last weeks of December and June and continuing for about a month.

Jo-Jo Outfitters

Hartenstraat, 23 (B2)
☎ 623 34 76
Spui
Trams 1, 2, 5
Open Mon. noon-6pm, Tue.-Fri. 11am-6pm.

British and American unlabelled brands for men, which are, however, clearly recognisable as designer wear. Quality and durability are the watchwords, with shirts, trousers and jackets from just €68 up to €182 for the best stuff. Nothing very imaginative, but they're all good quality items you can keep on wearing.

Lady Day

Hartenstraat, 9 (B2)
☎ 624 15 14
Open Mon.-Fri. 11am-6pm, Thu. until 9pm, Sun. 1-6pm.

Anyone with a penchant for retro clothing will be in heaven here. Most of the stock is vintage Americana from the 50s, 60s and 70s, and with evening dresses, suits, children's outfits and fashion accessories, you can kit out the whole family under one roof. Expect to pay between €30 and €32 for a shirt and no more than €36.50 for a pair of trousers.

Callas 43

Haarlemmerdijk, 43 (B1)
☎427 37 90
Spui
Trams 1, 2, 5
Open Mon.-Sat. noon-6pm.

Luxury secondhand gear, with clothing, jewellery and accessories by Karl Lagerfeld, YSL, Dior, Edgar Vos and other prestige brands for a third of the normal price. A very popular shop where you can find real bargains. Some think this alone justifies their trip. An address to keep under your hat.

Flea Market

Westerstraat (B2) and Noordermarkt (B1)
Open every Mon. 9am-1pm.

If you like rummaging around for a bargain, you'll be in your element here. All along

Westerstraat, you'll find stalls selling secondhand goods, such as fabrics, kitchenware and clothing. There's also a small flea market on Noordermarkt, where you can take your pick from Dutch chandeliers at bargain prices, wooden ice skates and heaps of fun knick-knacks.

John Fiets Inn

Spinozastraat, 2 (C/D3)
☎ 428 43 85
Metro Westerplein
Open Mon. 2-7pm, Tue.-Fri. 9am-7pm.

Sugar pink, leopard skin, with a child seat or a basket to carry your dog – however you like your bicycle, this is the place to find a bargain. Dutch *Gazelle* and *Batavus* bikes are on sale for around €130-134 secondhand (in other words half the price of a new model) and, unlike the market, you can be sure you're not buying a stolen vehicle here. If you really want to go Dutch, of course, you need one with a backpedal brake.

De Zwaan Saleroom

Keizersgracht, 68 (B1)
☎ 624 32 05.

You can buy absolutely anything from the city saleroom. The prices usually stay fairly low, so make sure you get some information about the date of the next sale before you arrive (some are held at the weekends). Items to be sold are put on display before the start of the auction, so you can examine a piece of furniture or other item that interests you at your leisure. Of course, it's better if you speak Dutch and don't put your hand up too rashly. To avoid surprises and make sure the item you want doesn't slip through your fingers, it's best to talk to the auctioneer before the sale starts.

Laura Dols en de Verkleed Komeet

Wolvenstraat, 7 (B2)
☎ 624 90 66
Open every day 11am-6pm, Thu. until 9pm, Sun. 2-6pm.

Here fans of 40s and 50s nostalgia will find everything they could

wish for to dress themselves from head to toe. From beautiful satin slips to a hat with a veil and matching gloves and handbag, there's an amazingly wide choice at amazingly low prices (crocodile-skin bag around €14, hat around €12). There's also loads of wonderful gift ideas, such as toilet requisites in a kid leather case, glittering costume jewellery and horn-rimmed sunglasses.

Second Best

Wolvenstraat, 18 (B2)
☎ 422 02 74
Open Mon. 1-6pm, Tue.-Fri. 11am-6pm, Sat. 11am-5pm.

Clothes that have hardly been worn, jettisoned by fashion photographers, designers and the idle rich when they're updating their wardrobes. In other words, this is absolutely *the* place to find that leather coat you've always dreamed of, a practically new pair of Prada shoes or some really wild lingerie. Allow €136-160 for an ensemble with a designer label, €73 for a leather jacket and €58 for a pair of trousers.

Zipper

Huidenstraat, 7 (B2)
☎ 623 73 02
Spui
Trams 1, 2, 5
Open Mon.-Sat. 11am-6pm, Thu. until 9pm, Sun. 1-5pm.

A great selection of clothing for 20-30 year-olds at amazing prices, with slightly-worn jeans, checked shirts, leather bomber jackets, little floral dresses and flares. At *Zipper* you can construct a total 70s look for next to nothing. Of course, if you're not young, or young-at-heart, you'd be better off going elsewhere.

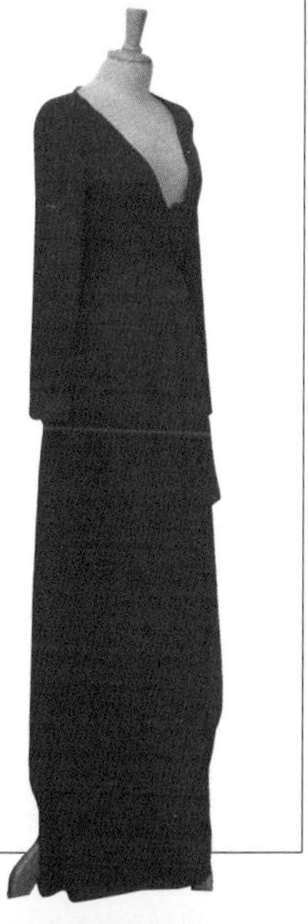

Nightlife Practicalities

Whether you're a music or theatre fan or just a night-owl, Amsterdam will fulfil all your expectations. Nightlife is concentrated in three districts, winter and summer.

Full of restaurants, theatres, bars and jazz clubs, Leidseplein is the haunt of young, fairly well-behaved people. In the red light district around the station, with its neon signs, women on display in shop windows, shady bars and countless sex shops, life goes on all night long, attracting a crowd of voyeuristic tourists, dealers and customers. But the real heartbeat of the Amsterdam nightlife can be heard around Rembrandtplein. This is where you'll find the coolest bars, the weirdest clubs and the wildest people, where gay revellers rub shoulders with students, foreigners and Amsterdam's upper crust, who can be observed out slumming it with the rest. Here too, if you want, you can dance all night long to the deafening sound of techno and house music.

As soon as the weather improves, the streets are filled with music and musical events, most of which can be enjoyed for free. There are open air rock, pop and jazz concerts and brass bands, particularly in Vondelpark and Amsterdamse Bos. Classical music also takes to the streets, settling on the barges moored along the canalsides or invading Jordaan.

Cafés

Around 8pm the beer and spirits start to flow. Barriers between different sections of society come down in the cafés, where Amsterdammers prefer to spend their evenings out, and where they can sit every night till 1am and as late as 2 or 3am on Friday and Saturday nights. From the unpretentious local cafés, where the customers sometimes break into song, to the 'brown cafés', where they drink strong beers with *jenever* chasers, to the cool cafés, where the young clubbers gather before going off to dance all night, to the coffee-shops where people drop in for a quick puff, to gay bars where leather gear is the rule, there's an enormous choice and you can easily move from one to another. They're all next to each other and you'll get a warm welcome in all of them.

Nightlife Amsterdam-Style

Don't bother with a classy wardrobe if you're going out in Amsterdam. The ambiance is relaxed

everywhere you go, and that goes for even the smartest, most prestigious places, such as the *Muziektheather* or *Concertgebouw*. Older people might want to wear an evening dress or a suit, but it's certainly not obligatory and you'll be allowed in without. You don't even have to wear a tie in the casino, though they do draw the line at shorts and trainers, and at the hippest clubs, the more original, unusual and cool you look, the more likely it'll be that the bouncer will let you in.

Discos and jazz clubs

The clubs open their doors at 11pm, but don't expect to find many people there that early. Before going to their favourite clubs, Amsterdammers take a tour of the cafés, setting off to dance around 1am and generally staying on till closing-time (4am on week nights and 5am on Friday and Saturday nights). It will cost you between €2.25 and €8 for entry, depending on what day it is, and no-one gets any special treatment. The door price sometimes includes the cost of a membership card, which enables you to go again another night. Bands start playing in the jazz clubs and music cafés around 9pm. You can get in for nothing as long as you buy drinks.

All year round there are concerts of every kind, from rock, pop and world music to classical and chamber music, as well as theatre, dance, opera and cabaret in a huge variety of places from the ordinary to the magnificent. To find the evening to suit you among the hundreds of events on offer each week, watch out for posters and read the monthly magazine *Uitkrant*, published by the AUB and available in bookshops, cafés and tourist information offices. It's published in Dutch, but provides a complete calendar of cultural events. There's a free supplement called *Pop & Jazz Uitlijst*, which comes out twice a week and gives you information on rock, blues and jazz concerts and what's on in the clubs. There's also an English-language *What's on*, published monthly by the VVV and providing day-by-day information on the main events on offer, including music, theatre and ballet. This is distributed free in all good hotels.

Tickets

Although the most prestigious early music concerts, operas and ballets are usually sold out weeks in advance, it's often possible to get tickets the day before, or on the night itself, though you shouldn't expect to get a very good seat.

Unless it's a last-minute decision, don't go to the concert hall or theatre to book your seats. The central booking office of the AUB (Amsterdams Uit Buro) Leidseplein, 26, near the Stadschouwburg, is open daily (including Sundays) 10am-6pm and until 9pm Thursdays. The €1.35 commission is also charged by the booking offices in the venues themselves and all credit cards are accepted. Remember that pre-booking for the same evening closes at 4pm. After that you have to go to the venue itself, where tickets are sold until an hour before the event starts. Seats that have been booked and paid for will be resold if not collected an hour before the curtain rises.

Booking tickets by phone

If you have a credit card, you can make a theatre or concert booking from your hotel by calling the Uitlijn, which is open daily. 9am-9pm ☎ 0900 0191 (€2.70 commision).

The VVV offices also handle bookings, but you have to go there in person. (Leidseplein, 106 or Stationplein, 10).

CONCERTS, THEATRE, CABARET, OPERA AND DANCE

Concertgebouw

Concertgebouwplein, 2-6
☎ 573 05 73
Trams 2, 3, 5, 12
Booking 10am-7pm
On-line booking: www.concertgebouw.nl
Tickets €13-40
Concerts at 8.15 or 8.30pm
For concerts sold out in advance, contact INFO-LINE ☎ 675 44 11, which provides information about seats available on the day.

This hall, renowned for the quality of its acoustics, is the home of the Royal Orchestra of the Netherlands, conducted by Riccardo Chailly. This temple to classical music stages concerts by the greatest early music ensembles, especially Baroque music.

Beurs Van Berlage

Damrak, 277 (B2/C1)
☎ 627 04 66
Booking Mon.-Sat. 12.30-6pm
Concerts begin at 8.30pm
Tickets €8.

This is the home of the Philharmonic orchestra of the Netherlands, as well as the National Orchestra of Chamber Music. Concerts by other classical music ensembles are also staged here, in the prestigious setting of a monument symbolic of the Dutch Art Nouveau movement.

Muziektheater

Amstel, 3 (B/C1)
☎ 625 54 55
Metro Waterlooplein
Booking Mon.-Sat. 10am-7pm
Concerts begin at 7.30pm or 8.15pm
Tickets €11-50.

The new Stopera complex, which opened in 1988, seats up to 1,600 spectators. The national ballet and the Netherlands Opera are based here and stage fairly eclectic programmes ranging from classical works to new productions.

Stadschouwburg

Leidseplein, 26 (A3)
☎ 523 77 00
Trams 1, 2, 5, 7, 10
Booking Mon.-Sat. 10am-6.30pm
Curtain rises at 8.15pm
Tickets €13-37.

The Stadschouwburg stages music concerts, as well as theatre and contemporary dance, performed by companies from the Netherlands and other countries.

Koninklijk Theater Carré

Amstel, 115-125 (B/C1)
☎ 622 52 25.

Since 1887 this former circus hall has provided a venue for grand spectaculars of all kinds, including circuses and a variety of musical shows.

Nieuwe de la Mar Theater

Marnistraat, 404 (A1)
☎ 530 53 02
Trams 7, 10.

This theatre specialises in cabaret and popular music and dance from all around the world.

De IJsbreker

Weesperzijde, 23 (C3)
☎ 668 18 05
Metro Weesperplein
Concerts begin at 8.30pm and 4.30pm on Sun.

This hall by the Amstel is the home of contemporary music (John Cage, Mauricio Kagel, Salvatore Sciarrino, Georg Katzer), with concerts of accordion and electronic music as well as various experimental groups.

Het Soeterijn

Linnaeusstraat, 2 (off map)
☎ 568 85 00
Trams 9, 14.

This little theatre attached to the Tropenmuseum prides itself on providing a stage for non-western culture. Its programme includes southern Moroccan, classical Arab and Indian music and Asian theatre and dance.

Felix Meritis Theatre

Keizersgracht, 324 (B2)
☎ 623 13 11
Trams 1, 2,5
Curtain rises at 8.30pm.

English-language avant-garde plays, as well as modern dance productions, are staged in the prestigious setting of this theatre, which first opened in 1787.

Nieuwe Kerk

Dam (B2)
☎ 638 69 09
Entry charge €6.80.

Every Sunday evening from July to the end of September there's a concert of organ music in the grand setting of the New Church. The programme includes works by Bach, Mendelssohn, Purcell and Buxtehude

Classical music concerts are also staged in Vondelpark, the English and Walloon churches of the Béguinage convent, the Van Loon museum, the Bethany cloister, St. Nicolas's church, the Oude Kerk and the large hall in the Tropenmuseum.

PLACE YOU BETS!

Holland Casino Amsterdam

Max Euweplein, 62 (A3)
☎ 620 10 06
Open daily 1.30pm-2am.
Entrance charge €2.70.

If you're tempted by the roulette wheel, Black Jack or poker, why not try the new casino near Leidseplein? The building is nothing special but the fever which grips the gamblers is the same as in older casinos. The café-restaurant on the lower floor has a lovely waterside terrace and stages cabaret shows from Wednesday to Sunday, starting at 6.30pm. You can also waltz to the sound of the orchestra.

A PICTURESQUE EVENING WALK IN THE AMSTELVELD

This lovely walk around the locality of bustling Rembrandtplein, where the many cafés stay open and busy late into the night, takes you along the canals and by the banks of the River Amstel, from which the city takes its name. What better way to explore Amsterdam after dark, than from the friendly buzz of the cafés and the quiet poetry of the silent canals?

STARTING FROM REMBRANDTPLEIN

This old square once housed the butter market and didn't receive its present name until the late 19th century, when a bronze statue of the famous 17th-century artist was erected in the centre. In summer the café terraces are full to bursting, and the competing sounds of music echo all round the square. Leave all this noise and bustle behind and take a stroll down Amstelsraat towards the Blue Bridge *(Blauwbrug)*.

THE BANKS OF THE AMSTEL

Instead of a canal, you come to the banks of a river, which has been lined with dykes because it flows below sea level here. The Blue Bridge (see p. 51), takes its name from the wooden bridge, painted blue, that used to cross the Amstel at this point. The bridge you see today dates from the end of the 19th century. Its finely-wrought candelabra stand on sculpted bases, representing the prows of ships.

Keep walking along the river bank in a southerly direction. After 300 m/yds you come to the Skinny Bridge *(Magere Brug)*, one of the last bascule bridges in the city and the one most loved by Amsterdammers. It was enlarged slightly when it was restored in 1969, but its shape remains largely unchanged. You can spot it easily at night by the lights along its arches and balancing arms.

PRINSENGRACHT

Keep walking along the river Amstel until you come to Prinsengracht – the Canal of Princes – and turn right to walk along it. After the river bank, which is always quite busy and lively, you suddenly plunge into a much calmer, quieter world, where it seems that everyone and everything is fast asleep.

The Dutch are less concerned with privacy than many other nations and many of their windows have neither shutters nor curtains. Even if you aren't usually given to voyeurism, when the lights come on take the opportunity to glance in at the interiors, which are often very tastefully decorated. An evening walk also enables you to spot some of the characteristic architectural features of houses in Amsterdam. For example, when people turn their lights on after dark, you can see the size of the windows. Often, at the front of the buildings, there's more glass than brick in order to let in as much daylight as possible. In the same way, as Amsterdam isn't a very sunny city, the windows are set flush with the wall, whereas in hotter places they tend to be more deeply recessed.

KOKADORUS AND AMSTELKERK

Cross Utrechtsestraat and keep walking along Prinsengracht until you come to the little square with the statue of Kokadorus, a famously silver-tongued stallholder who sold his wares in the little market held here until the beginning of the 20th century. Beside you you can see the Amstelkerk church, the oldest wooden church in Amsterdam. When it was built, it was intended to be a temporary measure, but was never replaced by a permanent structure as the clergy were unable to raise enough money to pay for it.

Go down Kerkstraat, which will take you back to Utrechtstraat. At the end of the street you'll see the bright lights of Rembrandtplein once more.

Cafés

As well as the cafés mentioned on p. 28-29, which stay open until 1-2am, here are some ideas for places which often have live music on Friday and Saturday nights, and where snacks and light meals are served until midnight or 1am.

De Engelbewaarder

Kloveniersburgwal, 57 (B/C2)
☎ 625 37 72
Open every day noon-1am, weekends until 3am.

There's a very relaxed atmosphere in this friendly café, which is the haunt of many newspaper people. Sunday is jazz day, when jazz-lovers come to enjoy the afternoon jam sessions.

De Twee Zwaantjes

Prinsengracht, 114 (B1)
☎ 625 27 29.

A typical Jordaan 'brown café' and former meeting-place for local brewers and workmen. Live music at weekends, or when the customers do the singing. A mixed crowd and very 'Jordaan' atmosphere – in other words working-class and fun.

Mulligan's

Amstel, 100 (B/C2)
☎ 622 13 30
Trams 4, 9, 14
Open every day 4pm-1am.

An atmosphere of heat and alcohol fumes in this Irish pub with live folk groups playing Celtic music at the weekends. Popular with the Irish, of course.

Dulac

Haarlemmerstraat, 118 (B1)
☎ 624 42 65
Bus 18, 22
Open every day 4pm-1am, weekends until 3am.

A large, smart café near the central station, decorated in a skilful blend of Art Deco and neo-Gothic, with live jazz groups on a Saturday night and Sunday afternoon.

Café Cox

Marnixstraat, 429 (A1)
☎ 620 72 22.

Favourite haunt of actors and directors from the *Stadschouwburg* next door. The kitchen is open until half-past midnight.

De Balie

Kleine Gartmanplantsoen, 10 (A3)
☎ 553 51 30
Open every day 11am-1am.

This large café, located near Leidseplein, is the locals' favourite stop after a visit to the cinema or theatre or before a night in a club. Snacks and light meals until 1am.

Van Puffelen

Prinsengracht, 375 (B2)
☎ 624 62 70
Open Mon.-Sat. 6-11pm, Sun. 5.30-10pm.

Cosy atmosphere, candlelight and, if you're peckish, light meals of Italian or French dishes.

Pop, Rock, Blues and Jazz Clubs

Alto Café

Korte Leidsedwarsstraat, 115 (Leidseplein, B3)
☎ 626 32 49
Open every night 9pm-3am, weekends until 4am.

Different types of band play live here, with a lively jam session on Wednesdays with Hans Dulfer, a pillar of the Amsterdam jazz scene. Hein van der Haag plays piano on Mondays.

Akhnaton

Nieuwezijds Kolk, 25 (B1)
☎ 624 33 96
Open Thu.-Sat. 10pm-5am, Sun. 2pm-7pm.

Fans of salsa, lambada and other Latino-African rhythms meet here every Friday. Live bands also play here.

Bamboo Bar

Lange Leidsedwarsstraat, 66 (B3)
☎ 624 39 93.

Jazz and blues bands play live every night after 10pm in pseudo tropical surroundings.

Bimhuis

Oudeschans, 73-77 (C2)
☎ 623 13 61
Metro Nieuwmarkt.

A temple to jazz, where great international jazz musicians come to play. Free jam sessions on Mondays, Tuesdays and Fridays. Tickets around €11 for live bands Thursday to Saturday.

Cruise Inn

Zeeburgerdijk, 271-273 (off map)
☎ 692 71 88.

Fans of good ol' 50s jive and rock 'n' roll gather here every Saturday night for some very acrobatic dancing.

Casablanca

Zeedijk, 26 (C1/2)
☎ 625 56 85
Open Mon.-Fri. 8pm-3am, weekends until 4am.

A jazz café with live bands Mondays to Wednesdays after 9pm. From Thursday to Saturday the place is given over to the joys of karaoke.

Paradiso

Weteringschans, 6-8 (A/B3)
☎ 626 45 21
(Leidseplein, A3).

When it ceased to be used as a church, this old building became the haunt of hippies, who came to sit in clouds of incense and marijuana smoke listening to Indian music. Now it's a venue for all kinds of music, from modern classical works to Mexican Mariachis, electronic, funk, jazz and salsa sounds. VIP nights on Fridays and *Paradisco* on Saturdays for those who still want to come here to dance.

De Westergasfabriek

Haarlemmerweg, 8-10 (off map)
☎ 581 04 25
Tram 10.

This former gasworks is now the venue for all kinds of cultural events themed around the future, with exhibitions, fashion shows, pop, rock and jazz bands and a discotheque in the *West Pacific* restaurant.

Melkweg

Lijnbaansgracht, 234 (A2)
☎ 624 17 77
(Leidseplein).

It's a sign of the times – this former dairy near Leidseplein, once the capital of 70s rock and a gathering-place for hippies, has had a total makeover. Today it's a venue for films, pop and world music gigs, avant-garde theatre productions and even a restaurant. For the nostalgic, there's a disco at weekends, with DJs hosting theme nights.

Blitz

Reguliersdwarsstraat, 45 (B2)
☎ 622 66 82.

A large aluminium bar with a dance-floor upstairs. A meeting-place for yuppies from all over, who come to drink explosive cocktails set alight in the glass. Good DJs on Thursday, Friday and Saturday nights.

NIGHTCLUBS

iT

Amstelstraat, 24 (C2)
Rembrandtplein.

The most outrageous club in Amsterdam where, once inside, you need to abandon all your inhibitions. House music and a very hot ambiance. A great place for posing, if that's what takes your fancy, but don't worry, you can just come to dance. Saturday is gay night.

More

Rozengracht, 133 (A2)
☎ 528 74 59
Open Mon.-Sat. 10pm-4am, closed Tue.

Upmarket hangout for young clubbers and arty bohemian types. Check listings as there's a different DJ every night. Rock, techno, funk – whatever you're into, you'll find it here.

Supperclub

Jonge Roelensteeg, 21 (B2)
☎ 638 05 13
Lounge-restaurant: open weekdays 8pm-1am, Fri.-Sat. until 2.30am; Club: open weekdays 7pm-1am, Fri.-Sat. until 4am.

This is *the* place to be right now. For around €55 you can dine lying down, propped up on huge pillows. Booking essential.

Odeon

Singel, 460 (behind flower market, B2).

The young, smart and comparatively staid come to this very cosy former residential home, with its painted ceilings and large mirrors. There's a choice of jazz in the cellar, retro music on the first floor and DJs in the hall of mirrors.

Escape-Chemistry

Rembrandtplein, 11 (B/C2/3).

The crowd consists mainly of teenagers at this mega disco. The ambiance depends on what the DJ's playing, but it's mostly somewhere between rap and the Smurfs, or commercial house music. Not for the over-30s!

Mazzo

Rozengracht, 114 (A2)
Trams 13, 14, 17.

Very relaxed ambiance with a young crowd who like urban dance music – rap, hip-hop, acid, and techno. London bands play live on Friday nights.

Havana

Reguliersdwarsstraat, 17-19 (behind the flower market, B2).

A bar and club where gays come together to drink, talk, meet people and dance the night away, after dinner until 1am, or 2am at weekends.

Soul Kitchen

Amstelstraat, 32 (C2)
Rembrandtplein.

For fans of 60s and 70s music, soul, funk and jazz in lovely surroundings. Membership card required.

Panama

Oostelijke Handelskade, 4 (C1/2)
☎ 311 86 86
Open Wed. and Thu. 10pm-3am, Fri. and Sat. midnight-4am.

Have dinner, dance, or watch a show. Different live music every night.

Understanding the menu

Common Dutch dishes

hutspot met klapstuk mashed potato with carrot, onion and beef
boerenkool met worst mashed potato with curly kale and smoked sausage
zuurkool met worst as above with sauerkraut instead of kale
andijviestamppot mashed potato with endive and meat
hachee met rode kool en appelmoes braised steak with onions and red cabbage and apple sauce
erwtensoep (snert) thick pea soup with ham
pannenkoek pancake
rijsttafel Indonesian 'rice table'
bittergarnituur platter of various snacks
vlammetjes little spicy vegetable spring rolls
bitterballen deep fried ragout in bread-crumbs, served with mustard
kroket as bitterballen but bigger, often eaten on bread
haring (Hollandse Nieuwe) fresh, raw herring
patatje oorlog chips served with mayonnaise, ketchup and peanut sauce
kaasplankje cheese platter; the most common cheese in Holland is 'Gouda' (*not* Edam)

Sweet dishes

poffertjes miniature pancakes served with powdery sugar and butter
zoete/zoute drop sweet/salty liquorice
stroopwafels syrup waffles
oliebollen Dutch doughnuts eaten around New Year
appelflappen apple doughnuts
speculaas Dutch biscuit baked with spices
ontbijtkoek breakfast cake with spices

Drinks

wine list wijnkaart
a cup of een kop
a glass of een glas
draught beer bier van de tap
mineral water Spa rood *(sparkling)*; Spa blauw *(still)*
fruit juice vruchtensap
milky coffee koffie verkeerd
decaffeinated coffee cafeïnevrije koffie
hot chocolate warme chocolademelk
hot aniseed milk warme anijsmelk
tea *(served weak and black)* thee *(pronounced: tay)*
herbal tea kruidenthee
strong tea with milk/lemon sterke thee met melk/citroen

General

rice rijst
egg ei (*plural:* eieren)
sugar suiker
salt/pepper zout/peper
mustard mosterd
oil olie

Meat

meat vlees
roast gebraad
baked gebakken in de oven
grilled gegrild
poached gepocheerd
steamed gestoomd
fried gebakken
deep fried gefrituurd
game wild
steak biefstuk
chop koteletje
veal kalfsvlees
ham ham
bacon spek or bacon
roast beef *(on bread)* rosbief

Fish and seafood

shellfish schaaldieren *or* schelpdieren
mussels mosselen
cod kabeljauw
salmon zalm
trout forel
sole tong
plaice schol
herring haring
monkfish zeeduivel
swordfish zwaardvis
tuna tonijn
shrimps/prawns garnalen
lobster kreeft
smoked eel gerookte paling

Vegetables

potato aardappel
tomato tomaat
curly kale boerenkool
thick carrot winterpeen
thin baby carrot worteltje
broad beans tuinbonen
endive andijvie
cauliflower bloemkool
sauerkraut zuurkool
red cabbage rode kool
beans bonen
leek prei
brussels sprouts spruitjes
pepper paprika

Fruit

fresh fruit vers fruit
orange sinaasappel
pear peer
apple appel
banana banaan
plums pruimen
grapes druiven
strawberries aardbeien
raspberries frambozen
blackberries bramen

Conversion tables for clothes shopping

Women's sizes

Shirts/dresses

U.K	U.S.A	EUROPE
8	6	36
10	8	38
12	10	40
14	12	42
16	14	44
18	16	46

Sweaters

U.K	U.S.A	EUROPE
8	6	44
10	8	46
12	10	48
14	12	50
16	14	52

Shoes

U.K	U.S.A	EUROPE
3	5	36
4	6	37
5	7	38
6	8	39
7	9	40
8	10	41

Men's sizes

Shirts

U.K	U.S.A	EUROPE
14	14	36
14½	14½	37
15	15	38
15½	15½	39
16	16	41
16½	16½	42
17	17	43
17½	17½	44
18	18	46

Suits

U.K	U.S.A	EUROPE
36	36	46
38	38	48
40	40	50
42	42	52
44	44	54
46	46	56

Shoes

U.K	U.S.A	EUROPE
6	8	39
7	9	40
8	10	41
9	10.5	42
10	11	43
11	12	44
12	13	45

More useful conversions

1 centimetre	0.39 inches	1 inch	2.54 centimetres
1 metre	1.09 yards	1 yard	0.91 metres
1 kilometre	0.62 miles	1 mile	1. 61 kilometres
1 litre	1.76 pints	1 pint	0.57 litres
1 gram	0.035 ounces	1 ounce	28.35 grams
1 kilogram	2.2 pounds	1 pound	0.45 kilograms

This guide was written by **Katherine Vanderhaeghe**
This edition was updated by Alix Delalande with the collaboration of Sandra Guinand, Élodie Louvet, Jean-Pierre Marenghi and Carine Merlin.
Translated by **Trista Selous**, additional translation **Jo Simons**.
Copy editor **Margaret Rocques.** Series editor **Sofi Mogensen**
Additional research and assistance: Christine Bell, Michael Summers, Kate Williams, Jenny Piening, Dave McCourt and Bernice Nikijuluw

We have done our best to ensure the accuracy of the information contained in this guide. However, addresses, phone numbers, opening times etc. inevitably do change from time to time, so if you find a discrepancy please do let us know. You can contact us at the address below.

Hachette Travel Guides provide independent advice. The authors and compilers do not accept any remuneration for the inclusion of any addresses in these guides.

Please note that we cannot accept any responsibility for any loss, injury or inconvenience sustained by anyone as a result of any information or advice contained in this guide.

Photo acknowledgements

Inside pages
Laurent Parrault: pp. 3 (t.l.; c.), 10 (c.r.), 12 (c.r.), 13 (t.r.; b.), 14, 15 (t.c.; c.r.; c.r. foreground), 16 (t.r.; b.r.), 17 (t.r.; b.), 18 (t.r.), 19 (t.l.; c.r.; b.r.), 20 (t.; b.), 21 (c.r.; c.l.; c.c.), 22 (t.; b.l.), 23 (t.c.), 24, 25 (t.l.; b.r.), 26 (c.c.), 27 (t.; b.l.), 28 (t.r.; b.l.), 30, 31, 32, 33, 38 (b.l.), 39, 40, 41 (c.l.; c.c.; b.l.; b.c.; b.r.), 42, 43, 45, 46, 47 (t.l.; b.l.; b.r.), 48, 49 (t.c.; b.l.; c.r.), 50, 51, 52, 53 (c.r. foreground; c.r.; c.l., b.c.), 54, 55, 56 (b.l.), 57, 58, 59 (t.r.; c.c.), 60 (c.r.; b.r.), 61, 62 (b.l.), 63 (t.l.; b.l.; b.r.), 64 (c.r.), 65, 66, 67 (t.l.; t.c.; t.r.; c.l.; c.c.), 68 (b.l.), 69, 71 (t.r.), 76 (b.l.), 77 (t.l.; c.r.), 78 (t.l.; c.c.; b.r.), 79 (c.l.), 80 (c.l.; c.c.), 81 (c.l.; c.r.; b.c.), 86 (t.r.; b.r.), 87, 88 (t.c.; c.l., b.c.), 89 (t.l., c.c.), 90, 91, 92, 93, 94 (t.r.; c.r.), 95, 96 (t.l.; t.r.; b.c.; b.l.), 97, 98, 99, 100 (t.r.; t.l.; b.r.), 101 (t.l.; c.c.; b.r.), 102, 103, 104 (t.r.; b.l.; b.r.), 105, 106 (b.l.), 107, 108, 109 (t.l.; t.c.; t.r.; c.r.; b.r.), 110 (t.r.; b.c.), 111 (c.c. foreground), 112 (t.r.; c.c.), 113 (c.l.; c.r.; b.c.), 114, 115 (c.r.), 119, 121 (b.r.), 122 (t.r.), 123 (b.r.), 124 (b.r.). **Christian Sarramon**: pp. 2 (t.c.), 3 (b.r.), 12 (t.c.; b.c.), 13 (c.l.), 16 (c.c.), 17 (c.r.), 18 (c.r.; b.l.), 19 (t.c.), 20 (c.r.), 22 (c.c.), 23 (b.r.), 26 (t.r.), 27 (c.l.; c.r.), 28 (c.r.), 29 (t.l.; c.l.), 38 (b.r.), 53 (t.c.), 56 (c.r.; b.r.), 59 (c.r.; b.l.; b.r.), 60 (b.l.), 64 (b.l.), 72 (t.r.), 75 (t.r.), 80 (b.r.), 101 (t.r.), 106 (t.r.; c.r.), 109 (c.c.), 110 (c.l.), 111 (t.l.; t.r.; b.r.), 112 (c.r.), 118, 120, 121 (t.l.; c.l.). **Katherine Vanderhaeghe**: p. 17 (t.l.). **Éric Guillot:** p. 115 (t.c.). **Hachette:** pp. 10 (t.c.), 10-11 (b.), 11, 13 (t.c.;©), 15 (b.l.), 21 (b.r.), 44 (b.l.;©), 47 (c.c.), 62 (c.r.), 63 (c.l.;©). **Smokiana**: p. 21 (t.). **De Gouden Reael**: p. 67 (c.l.). **Canal House**: p. 73 (b.l.). **Ambassade Hotel**: p. 73 (b.r.). **Toro Hotel**: p. 75 (b.). **De Roode Leeuw**: p. 76 (c.c.). **Le Pêcheur**: p. 78 (b.l.). **Le Garage**: p. 79 (t.c.). **Zabar's**: p. 79 (t.r.). **The Pancake Bakery**: p. 80 (t.r.). **De Admiraal**: p. 81 (c.c.). **Fever**: p. 86 (c.l.). **Van Heek**: p. 88 (c.r.). **Eva Damave**: p. 89 (b.r.). **Riviera**: p. 94 (c.l.). **Kashba**: p. 96 (b.r.). **Pakhuis Amsterdam**: p. 100 (b.l.). **What's cooking**: p. 104 (c.r.). **Unlimited Delicious** © Peter Schut: p. 113 (t.r.). **Second Best**: p. 115 (b.r.).

Front cover
Image Bank– Bokelberg: t.c.; **Image Bank–David de Lossy**: b.c.; **Christian Sarramon**: c.l., c.c., c.r., br.; **Laurent Parrault**: t.l., b.l.; **Pix V.C.L.**: c. r (foreground).

Back cover
Christian Sarramon: t.r., c.l.; **Laurent Parrault**: c. (foreground), b.l.

Illustrations: Pascal Garnier **Cartography** © Hachette Tourisme

English edition © Hachette UK 2002. Reprinted 2003
French edition © Hachette Livre (Hachette Tourisme) 2001

All rights reserved. No part of this publication may be reproduced in any material form (including photocopying or storing it in any medium by electronic means and whether or not transiently or incidentally to some other use of this publication) without the written permission of the copyright owner, except in accordance with the provisions of the Copyright, Designs and Patents Act 1988 or under the terms of a licence issued by the Copyright Licensing Agency, 90 Tottenham Court Road, London W1P 9HE. Application for the copyright holder's permission to reproduce any part of this publication should be addressed to the publisher.

Distributed in the United States of America by Sterling Publishing Co., Inc.
387 Park Avenue South, New York, NY 10016-8810

A CIP catalogue for this book is available from the British Library

ISBN 184202 145 1

Hachette Travel Guides, c/o Philip's, 111 Salusbury Road, London NW6 6RG

Printed and bound in Slovenia

STAYING ON A LITTLE LONGER

If you're staying for a few days and would like to try some new places, the following pages give you a wide choice of hotels, restaurants and bars, listed by district with addresses.
Although you can just turn up at a restaurant and have a meal (except in the most prestigious establishments), don't forget to book your hotel several days in advance (see page 70).
Enjoy your stay!

The prices quoted here are for a double room with en-suite bathroom or shower and include breakfast and local tax at 5%, but are a guide only. It's useful to know that in four and five-star hotels breakfasts are quite expensive (around €14), but it's possible to book a room exclusive of breakfast. Prices shown are those that apply in high season though they may be subject to increases or reductions. It's also useful to know that many of the luxury hotels used by businessmen during the week reduce their charges at weekends. If you'd like to stay in an old-style hotel, make sure you book at least two months in advance.

For more detailed information see Rooms and Restaurants (p. 70).

Centraal Station

Golden Tulip Barbizon Palace*****
Prins Hendrikkade, 59-72
☎ 556 45 64
Ⓕ 624 33 53
From €265-325,
breakfast €19.
A modern hotel, with an international clientele, occupying a group of 17th-century houses on the edge of the red light district. There's a conference room in the St Olof Chapel and the restaurant has been awarded stars, but the rooms vary greatly, the ones in the old houses being preferable as they're better equipped and have views over the IJ. Perfect service.

Renaissance*****
Kattengat, 1
☎ 621 22 23
Ⓕ 627 52 45
Around €263.
An extremely large hotel complex (405 rooms), with an international clientele, and a 'brown café', disco, several restaurants and even a Lutheran church. Benefits from a very central location. Car park for patrons.

Victoria****
Damrak, 1-5
☎ 623 42 55/627 11 66
Ⓕ 625 29 97/627 42 59
Around €250,
breakfast €17.
A neo-Classical luxury hotel opposite the station, dating from 1890, with 305 huge, luxurious rooms, all double-glazed. Attractions include beautiful marble decor, stained-glass windows, a covered terrace with panoramic view and a fitness centre with swimming-pool and sauna.

Amstel Botel***
Oosterdokskade, 2-4
☎ 626 42 47
Ⓕ 639 19 52
Around €79,
breakfast €6.80.
A large white ship moored near the central station, with 176 rather narrow but well-equipped cabins at reasonable prices. An unusual way to stay in the midst of Amsterdam's houseboats. Ask for a cabin overlooking the IJ as the quayside view isn't that great.

Dam

Krasnapolsky*****
Dam, 9 (trams 4-9-16-20)
☎ 554 91 11
Ⓕ 622 86 07
Around €290,
breakfast €19.50.
Magnificent 19th-century hotel opposite the royal palace, with an immense garden where meals are served any time of day. Boasts 429 luxury rooms and a car park with 150 places, which is very useful in this district.

Amsterdam****
Damrak, 93-94 (trams 4-9-16-20)
☎ 555 06 66
Ⓕ 620 47 16
Around €190,
breakfast €13.60.
One of Amsterdam's old hotels near the Dam, now entirely renovated by the Best Western chain. Very good value for money and the ground-floor restaurant serving Dutch specialities, De Rode Leeuw, *won the* Neerlands Dis *prize.*

Die Port Van Cleve****
Nieuwezijds Voorburgwal, 176-180 (trams 1-2-5)
☎ 624 48 60
Ⓕ 622 02 40
From €192-295,
breakfast €14.70.
Located behind the royal palace and the Magna Plaza shopping centre, this hotel is worth rediscovering, particularly since the renovation of its brasserie De Poort, *which serves authentic Dutch cuisine. The rooms have also been modernised.*

Rembrandt Residence***
Herengracht, 255
(trams 13-17-20)
☎ 622 17 27
Ⓕ 625 06 30
Around €159,
breakfast included.
A very cosy hotel occupying a group of 17th and 18th-century houses and admirably situated on the magnificent Herengracht, between Jordaan and the Dam. One of the best hotels in Amsterdam for those who want luxury hotel service at an affordable price.

Rho***
Nes, 11-23
☎ 620 73 71
Ⓕ 620 78 26
From €113-146,
breakfast included.
Sadly the conversion of this old Art Deco theatre does not extend beyond the vast foyer. The best of the 160 functionally-furnished rooms are at the back. Use of private car park for an additional charge.

The Béguinage and Rokin

Doelen****
Nieuwe Doelenstraat, 24
(trams 4-9-16-20)
☎ 554 06 00
Ⓕ 622 10 84
Around €206.
One of the city's oldest hotels, where Sissi and Sarah Bernhardt stayed. The rooms are a little disappointing but the breakfast

room overlooking the Amstel and the Belle Époque lounges are lovely. The best rooms (some with balconies) are at the back on the first and second floors.

City Centre Hotel***
Nieuwezijds Voorburgwal, 50 (trams 1-2-5)
☎ 422 00 11
Ⓕ 420 03 57
Around €149, breakfast included.
Modernism and functionalism are the watchwords in this hotel, which has a lovely coloured façade. Close to the university and Spui, good value for money for those who don't like guesthouses.

Nes***
Kloveniersburgwal, 137-139 (trams 4-9-16-20)
☎ 624 47 73
Ⓕ 620 98 42
Around €134.
A lovely Baroque gabled façade hides this little hotel by the side of a quiet canal behind Doelen. Its 36 rooms have recently been renovated and furnished with every convenience. Ask for a view over the Amstel. The restaurants and bars of Rembrandtplein are just a 5-minute walk away.

Rokin**
Rokin, 73 (trams 4-9-16-20)
☎ 626 74 56
Ⓕ 625 64 53
Around €98, breakfast included.
Very small and basic, but pleasant. About half the rooms have en-suite bathrooms or a view of the canal. Usually a fairly young clientele.

Rembrandtplein

Schiller****
Rembrandtplein, 26-36 (trams 4-9)
☎ 554 07 00
Ⓕ 624 00 98
Around €190, breakfast €12.50.
This Art Deco gem, restored in 1997, has at last regained the brilliance it had when it was first built in 1912 by Fritz Schiller, an amateur painter and art lover. Cosy lounges, 92 tastefully decorated rooms and a superb brasserie which is one of the favourite meeting-places of Amsterdam's high society.

Jolly Hotel Carlton****
Vijzelstraat, 4 (trams 16-24-25)
☎ 622 22 66
Ⓕ 626 61 83
From €136-454, breakfast included.
Italian-style hospitality in this fine brick building overlooking Munttoren, with Murano lights, marble decor and designer furniture. Good food and comfortable rooms with en-suite bathrooms, some with a lovely view. Additional charge for use of the garage.

Canal Crown****
Herengracht, 519-525 (trams 16-24-25)
☎ 420 00 55
Ⓕ 420 09 93
From €159-191, breakfast €11.30.
This hotel on the corner of Vijzelstraat and Herengracht was renovated in 1993. It has 56 very pleasant rooms with en-suite bathrooms. Double glazing guarantees quiet nights. Perfect service and a 24-hour bar.

Eden***
Amstel, 144 (trams 9-20)
☎ 530 78 78
Ⓕ 623 32 67
From €134-192, breakfast €12.50.
A small hotel by the Amstel, managed by Best Western, very modern and tastefully decorated. The rooms overlooking the river have a magnificent view but are a little more expensive.

Amsterdam Prinsengracht***
Prinsengracht, 1015 (trams 4-20)
☎ 623 77 79
Ⓕ 623 89 26
From €100-134, breakfast included.
A comfortable hotel not far from the Van Loon museum, in the 'bourgeois' district of Prinsengracht. There's a small garden at the back and all rooms are provided with en-suite shower and toilet.

Mercure Arthur Frommer***
Noorderstraat, 46
(trams 16-24-25)
☎ 622 03 28
Ⓕ 620 32 08
Around €141,
breakfast €12.50.
The rooms are comfortable but a little cramped and the breakfast room is rather dark. However, the hotel benefits from a quiet location and has a very reasonably-priced car park. Ten minutes walk from the district with the best clubs in Amsterdam, and the flower market.

Leidseplein

Maas***
Leidsekade, 91
(trams 1-2-5)
☎ 623 38 68
Ⓕ 622 26 13
Around 143,
breakfast included.
A small, comfortable hotel not far from the large museums and the bustle of Leidseplein. It has some lovely rooms overlooking the canal and you can enjoy the water beds and whirlpools. Baby-sitting service and generous breakfast.

Terdam***
Tesselschadestraat, 23
(trams 1-2-5)
☎ 612 68 76
Ⓕ 683 83 13
From €141-154,
breakfast included.
Although the Viennese decor is confined to the lobby, this is a pleasant hotel, well located in a comparatively quiet street for the district. And no one will get jealous as the rooms are all the same.

Nieuwmarkt

The Grand*****
Oudezijds Voorburgwal, 197 (trams 4-9-16-20)
☎ 555 31 11
Ⓕ 555 32 22
Around €375,
breakfast €18.50.
In the 16th century this former city hall of Amsterdam was a royal residence. It's now converted into a luxury hotel, ideally located in the heart of the city. After a day's sightseeing you'll appreciate the heated pool, sauna and Turkish bath. Private car park and a good brasserie.

Plantage

Lancaster***
Plantage Middenlaan, 48
(trams 9-14)
☎ 626 65 44
Ⓕ 622 66 28
Around €148,
breakfast €10.50.
This hotel opposite the Artis zoo has 88 comfortable rooms, though with unoriginal decoration. Guests tend to be young and international.

Rembrandt**
Plantage Middenlaan, 17
(trams 9-14)
☎ 627 27 14
Ⓕ 638 02 93
Around €70.
This guesthouse in a 19th-century patrician house in a very leafy district is a stone's throw from Waterlooplein. Ideal for those on low budgets and families (some rooms have 4 beds). Of the 16 rooms only 9 have en-suite shower and toilet. Those overlooking the garden are the most quiet.

The museum quarter

The Park***
Stadhouderskade, 25
(trams 6-7-10)
☎ 671 12 22
Ⓕ 664 94 55
Around €159.
This hotel offers 4-star service at an affordable price, with pretty, comfortable rooms and a central location near the Rijksmuseum, sight-seeing boats and antique shops. Private car park.

Fita***
Jan Luykenstraat, 37
(trams 2-5-20)
☎ 679 09 76
Ⓕ 664 39 69
Around €129,
breakfast included.
A quiet little hotel run by a pleasant couple. Sixteen large, light rooms with the latest in en-suite bathrooms, and a breakfast room in the basement. There are parking facilities in the area.

Aalders***
Jan Luykenstraat, 13-15
(trams 2-5-20)
☎ 672 46 98
Ⓕ 662 01 16
Around €102.
A favourite hotel for music-lovers because of its proximity to the Concertgebouw and museums. There's a very pleasant breakfast room, the bedrooms are light and spacious and the welcome is excellent.

Acro**
Jan Luykenstraat, 44
(trams 2-5-20)
☎ 662 55 38
Ⓕ 675 08 11
Around €82,
breakfast included.
Two early 20th-century houses in a residential district a stone's throw from Vondelpark, the large museums and shopping streets, have been converted into a functional hotel offering comfortable rooms at a very reasonable price.

De Pijp

La Richelle***
Holbeinstraat, 41 (trams 5-24)
☎ 671 79 71
Ⓕ 671 05 41
From €134-180,
breakfast €11.
Although it's some way from the centre, this little hotel will please those who like a family welcome and beautiful location. Spacious rooms (some duplexes), light colours, antiques, Persian carpets and a small, typically Dutch garden full of flowers. Private car park for an additional charge and it's also possible to park in the street.

Don't forget to see pages 72–75 for more hotels.

HOTELS

Generally speaking, the Dutch eat dinner early. Restaurants open from 6pm and kitchens tend to close around 10pm. Prices shown here are a guide only but include 15% service. For more information about opening hours, booking and prices, see Rooms and Restaurants Practicalities (p. 70).

Centraal Station

Lana-Thai
Warmoesstraat, 10
☎ 624 21 79
Open Tue.-Sun. 5-11pm
Set menus €23-46.
Stunning decor, including furniture and rich fabrics imported from Thailand, which fits perfectly with the authentic, highly-spiced cuisine. Don't miss the green curry and penang kung.

Vermeer
Prins Hendrikkade, 59-72
☎ 556 45 64
Open Mon.-Fri. noon-3pm, 6.30-10pm,
Sat. 6.30-10pm only
Set menu €60.
Truly excellent food, cosy decor and perfect service. The highly inventive, exclusively French cuisine is accompanied by carefully selected wines. Booking advisable. Free parking.

Dam

Dorrius
Nieuwezijds Voorburgwal, 5
☎ 420 22 24
Open every day 5.30-11pm.
Dark wood panelling on the walls and ceiling, tiles out of a Vermeer painting, old stained-glass windows and moulded glass light fittings. This historic restaurant, dating from 1890 and totally renovated, serves Dutch cuisine. Each month a different province is highlighted, so you might find mussels from Zeeland, asparagus from Limburg or pheasant from the east. Succulent dishes served in regional crockery.

Lieve
Herengracht, 88
☎ 624 96 35
Open every day 7.30-10.30pm
Set menu €22.50.
Fish specialities and some meat dishes, particularly game in season, cooked in the best traditions of Belgian gastronomy, inspired by Pierre Wijnants. A very popular place, no doubt because of its unforgettable shrimp croquettes and crab bisque, and as an accompaniment, one of the fine wines on the list, or a robust beer.

Jordaan

Cervejaria Alcantara
Westerstraat, 184-186
☎ 420 39 59
Open every day 6-11pm
From €14 (no credit cards).
The setting is like a fish market, with bright lights and the kitchen located in the restaurant itself. Here you can sample enhanced Portuguese cuisine. This place is still very trendy and therefore always busy.

Cilubang
Runstraat, 10
☎ 626 97 55
Open Tue-Sun. 6-11pm
Set menu €22.50.
If you like to pick at lots of different dishes at once and you truly love Indonesian food, then go and order a rijsttaffel in this little restaurant that doesn't look like very much from the outside, but where the food is excellent.

Duende
Lindengracht, 62
☎ 420 66 92
Open every day 4pm-1am, Fri.-Sat. until 3am
Tapas €2.30-4.00.
More than a tapas bar, a little restaurant decorated with Andalusian ceramics. It's hard to choose between the 17 different tapas dishes, not to mention the dishes of the day, all washed down with a robust Spanish wine. There's a flamenco show at the back once a month and live music every Saturday.

Koevoet
Lindenstraat, 17
☎ 624 08 46
Open Tue.-Sat. 6-11pm.
A little workers' restaurant almost unchanged since 1850, with simple food, a convivial ambiance and house wine. Nothing extraordinary about the food, but enjoy the slice of Jordaan life.

Sancerre
Reestraat, 28-32
☎ 627 87 94
Open every day 6-10.30pm
Set menu €28.40.
French cuisine with herbs, wines from the Loire, fine Art Deco interior and perfect service. A high-quality restaurant, competitively priced. Vegetarian dishes available.

Takens
Runstrat, 17d
☎ 627 06 18
Open every day 6-10.30pm
Set menus from €24.
Edwin Takens loves subtle food, combining tastes and trends with a few exotic touches. Don't miss the shrimp bouillon with truffles or grilled steak with smoked oysters. Yet more surprises in the 6 set meals, which change weekly, and excellent wines.

Spui

D'Vijff Vlieghen
Spuistraat, 294-302
☎ 624 83 69
Open every day 5.30-10.30pm
Set menu €25.
The decor hasn't changed for three hundred and fifty years, with chequered tiles, gilded wallpaper, carved oak panelling and a labyrinth of cosy rooms where you can eat Dutch nouvelle cuisine based on fish, seafood and vegetables in season.

Luden
Spuistraat, 304-306
☎ 622 89 79
Open every day 6-10.30pm
Set menus from €25.
A Parisian-style brasserie of the kind Amsterdammers love, the

more so since it's one of the few restaurants with two sittings, at 6 and 9pm. Good if unsurprising, French-inspired food. Always packed, especially at weekends.

Leidseplein

Raffle's Steakhouse
Kleine Gartmanplantsoen, 5
☎ 638 72 20
Open every day 9am-2am
Dishes €4.50-9.00
Warm Latin-American decor in blues and browns for lovers of good, charcoal-grilled Argentinian meat. BBQs, spare ribs, 500g/1lb steaks for the hungry, and empanadas and fish in season. Try the Uruguayan-style mussels and Chilean and Argentinian wines.

't Swarte Schaep
Korte Leidsedwarsstraat, 24
☎ 622 30 21
Open every day for lunch and dinner
Set meals €38-57.
Buried among the fast food outlets, this traditional restaurant is on the first floor of a house dating from 1687. Black pudding, lobster and good wines. A little expensive, but very good quality.

De Oesterbar
Leidseplein, 10
☎ 626 34 63
Open every day for lunch and dinner
Set menus €34-36.
If you like fish, you'll love this restaurant entirely dedicated to seafood. Maatjes *(marinated herrings) with onions, shrimps, oysters and eels, which you can eat at the bar at the back, or bigger dishes to eat round the table with a glass of iced jenever.*

Rembrandtplein

Les Quatre Canetons
Prinsengracht, 1111
☎ 624 63 07
Open Mon.-Fri. lunch and dinner, Sat. dinner only
Set menu €31.50.
As its French name suggests, this is the place to eat duck, duck with red peppers, foie gras and many other recipes invented by Jacques Roosebrand, who loves the food of south-west France. Good wine list.

Kort
Amstelveld, 12
☎ 626 11 99
Open every day 11.30am-midnight.
Set menu €23.
Jim Kort opened his restaurant in the basement of the oldest wooden church in Amsterdam. Post-modern decor, French nouvelle cuisine and trendy clientele. When the sun shines they put out tables under the walnut trees on the charming little square.

Panini
Vijzelgrachr, 3-5
☎ 626 49 39
Open every day 9am-11pm
Dishes from €6.80.
A lunchtime snack of Tuscan panini and salad, or a more relaxed evening meal of fresh pasta, gamberetti and escalopes, washed down with a glass of chianti. Even with no sun you'll think you're in Italy as the ingredients and cuisine are 100% Italian.

Piet de Leeuw
Noorderstraat, 11
☎ 623 71 81
Open every day noon-11pm, dinner only Sat. and Sun.
Dishes from €8.60.
A typically Dutch restaurant frequented mainly by locals who eat good grilled steak, fresh sole or eels on toast at large buffet tables. Conviviality guaranteed.

De Pijp

Quinto
Frans Halsstraat, 42
☎ 679 68 48
Open every day 6-11pm
Dishes from €11.
If you're staying in this rather remote district of Amsterdam, you'll be very pleased to find this authentic café-restaurant with its warm decor of wood. Large

convivial tables and a fairly limited menu that's full of great surprises. As well as the traditional hutspot you'll find ostrich and exotic fish. Besides which, it's a really friendly place.

Further afield

Amsterdam
Watertorenplein, 6
(terminus of tram 10)
☎ 682 26 66
Open every day
11.30am–11.30pm
Dishes from €11.
The trendy new brasserie you mustn't miss, in a vast warehouse lit by big lights from the old Ajax stadium. Large and small meals all day, good wines, a good ambiance and good prices. Essential.

La Rive (Hotel Amstel)
Prof Tulpplein, 1 (trams 6-7-10)
☎ 622 60 60
Open every day noon-10pm, dinner only Sat. and Sun.
Certainly expensive, but succulent and unforgettable. If you want to treat yourself to a real gourmet meal, don't miss this truly wonderful restaurant overlooking the Amstel, particularly in summer when the terrace is open.

CAFÉ-RESTAURANTS

Nieuwmarkt

Dantzig
Zwanenburgwal, 15
☎ 620 90 39
Open every day 9am-1am.
Before or after your visit to the next-door Stopera, the largest terrace in town, by the side of the Amstel, and a wide range of large and small dishes at very affordable prices. Smart decor, mixed clientele.

In de Waag
Nieuwmarkt, 4
☎ 422 77 72
Open every day
10am-1am.
In the very fine, spare setting of the old St. Anthony dock you can lunch with the dish of the day, dine by candlelight with something more, or just have a real espresso. A truly exceptional terrace on a square in one of the nicest districts of Amsterdam.

Dam

Het Paleis
Paleisstraat, 16
☎ 626 06 00
Open every day 11am-1am and until 2am
Fri. and Sat.
In this café close to the palace, Inge and Babette will give you a royal reception, whether it's for a quick snack or a slow drink. In summer the large terrace by the water's edge is fit for a king.

Villa Zeezicht
Torensteeg, 7
Open every day 8am-7pm, 9am-7pm at weekends.
At this café, with its superb view of one of the city's largest bridges and its tables outside in fine weather, you can have cakes or savoury snacks, tea and Italian coffee. Service provided entirely by women, all very nice and friendly.

Jordaan

Café Nielsen
Berenstraat, 19
☎ 330 60 06
Open Tue.-Sat. 8.30am-5pm, Sun. 9.30am-5pm.
For those who'd rather have their breakfast or brunch in a café than at the hotel, real Italian coffee broodjes *(rolls), lovely salads and home-made tarts, all served by a very friendly couple.*

Don't forget to look on page 125 for restaurant vocabulary and menu translator.

RESTAURANTS

Young people in Amsterdam meet up in cafés and bars before setting off to dance the night away in clubs. For more information on what's going on, what to wear and opening hours, turn to Nightlife Practicalities (see pages 116-117).

BARS AND CAFÉS

Centraal Station

Latei
Zeedijk, 143
☎ 625 74 85
Open Mon.-Thu. 8am-7pm, Fri. and Sat. until 10pm.
If you're desperate to take home the crockery your breakfast was served on, no problem, you can have it for a few florins, because everything's for sale here, including the furniture. But don't let that distract you from finishing your delicious apple tart!

Mooy
Kolksteeg,14
☎ 624 02 94
Open every day noon-1am.
Mooy has been here since 1620 and is still going strong among the local sex shops and dens of ill repute. It has a traditional Amsterdam café decor of Delft tiles, copper light fittings and a rather old-fashioned air – which also applies to some of the customers.

Dam

Ter Kuile
Torensteeg, 8
☎ 639 10 55
Open every day 11am–1am, Fri. and Sat. until 3am.
A new generation 'brown café', with Art Deco lamps and lovely wrought iron. Frequented by the young and hip or the laid back and located in a pleasant part of town between Dam and Jordaan. Snacks and light meals served all day.

Leidseplein

Het Hok
Lange Leidsedwarsstraat, 134
☎ 624 31 33
Open every day 9am-1am.
Cosy ambiance and maximum concentration around the chess board. A locals' café where, despite the mental battles at hand, they don't forget to raise their glasses, or laugh and talk between games.

Spui

Café Gollem
Raamsteeg, 4
Open every day 10am-1am.
The café for lovers of Belgian beer, with nine different draught beers and 200 bottled varieties available.

De Still
Spuistraat, 326
☎ 620 13 49
Open Sun.-Thu. 1pm-1am, Fri. and Sat. until 3am.
A pub-style café specialising in whisky. An unbelievable choice of blends and malts from around the world, including Japan.
A great place to meet before or after dinner.

Jordaan

Café Tabac
Brouwersgracht, 101 (corner of Prinsengracht)
☎ 622 44 13
Open every day 10.30am-1am, Fri. and Sat. until 3am
Wooden benches and bar, tobacco coloured walls, quiet and cosy during the day, very busy at night. Here you can have a late breakfast, a good draught beer or sit outside for a drink before dinner in summer.

De Koophandel
Bloemgracht, 49
Open Sun.-Thu. 10pm-3am, Fri.-Sat. 10pm-4am.
This café, housed in a former Jordaan warehouse, is also a meeting place where occasional exhibitions are held. Live music at weekends and snacks and light meals all day long.

Thijssen
Brouwersgracht, 107 (corner of Lindengracht)
☎ 623 89 94
Open Mon.-Fri. 9am-1am, Sat. 7am-2.30am.
This new generation 'brown café' near Noordermarkt, larger and with a more designer look than the older ones, is decorated with magnificent Art Deco lamps. Very busy on Saturdays, which is market day, and Friday nights. Wide choice of delicious rolls served during the day.

See page 122 for more late night cafés and bars.

NIGHTCLUBS

The Supperclub
Jonge Roelensteeg, 21
Open Wed.-Sun. 7pm-2/3am.
The latest, hippest pre-club bar in a dark little street near the Dam, where you can eat or drink to sounds mixed by the best DJs. An essential stop before you dive into one of Amsterdam's hottest clubs.

Sinners in Heaven
Wagenstraat, 3-7 (Plantage)
Open Thu.-Sun. 10pm-2/3am.
The new temple of dance and glamour on 3 floors with 3 different ambiances: church, chateau or dungeon. Special sinners' night every Sunday.

Margarita's
Regulierdwarsstraat, 108-114
Open Wed.-Sun. 9pm-2/3am.
Black magic vinyl groove with a dash of Latino. Dance to Caribbean rhythms on Saturday, salsa on Sunday.

Dansen bij Jansen
Handboogstraat, 11
☎ 620 17 79
Open every day 11pm-4am.
A disco purely for students, who dance the night away like maniacs to house music. Photos by the entrance give you an idea of how to dress to please the doorman. Not for over-25s.

Exit
Regulierdwarsstraat, 42
☎ 625 87 88
Open every day 7pm-1/3am.
A very popular gay club. Great music for dancing.

Time
Nieuwezijds Voorburgwal, 163-5
Open Tue-Sun 10pm-4am
Admission €4.50, free before 11pm.
New, smart looking club with mirrors and a long bar which attracts a young crowd. Tuesday is reggae night, Wednesday is the popular drum and bass night. Rest of the week features house and dance music.

More
Rozengracht, 133
☎ 528 74 59
Open Wed.-Sun. 10pm-3/4am
Housed in the former Roothaanhuis, this bright club, with its white walls and pink floor, has plenty of room for dancing. Each week there's a different theme with house DJs and acts providing the entertainment. Every Wednesday night is gay night. Cover charge €6.75.

Paradiso
details on page 123 and
De Melkweg
details on page 124
Although already featured earlier in the guide, these two clubs deserve a mention here, as their dance nights at the weekends are extremely popular and very trendy.

See pages 123–124 for more clubs and live music.

NOTES

NOTES

HACHETTE TRAVEL GUIDES

A GREAT WEEKEND IN ...

Amsterdam	1 84202 145 1
Barcelona	0 54008 323 2
Berlin	1 84202 061 7
Brussels	1 84202 017 X
Budapest	0 54008 274 0
Dublin	1 84202 096 X
Florence	0 54008 322 4
Lisbon	1 84202 011 0
London	1 84202 168 0
Madrid	1 84202 095 1
Naples	1 84202 016 1
New York	0 54008 321 6
Paris	1 84202 001 3
Prague	1 84202 000 5
Rome	1 84202 169 9
Seville	0 54008 275 9
Venice	1 84202 018 8
Stockholm	0 54008 318 6
Vienna	1 84202 026 9

ROUTARD

Indulge your taste for travel with the ultimate food, drink and accommodation guides for the independent traveller.

Andalucia & Southern Spain	1 84202 028 5
Athens & the Greek Islands	1 84202 023 4
Belgium	1 84202 022 6
North Brittany	1 84202 020 X
California, Nevada & Arizona	1 84202 025 0
Canada	1 84202 031 5
Cuba	1 84202 062 5
Ireland	1 84202 024 2
Paris	1 84202 027 7
Provence & the Côte d'Azur	1 84202 019 6
Rome & Southern Italy	1 84202 021 8
Thailand	1 84202 029 3

VACANCES

Colourful, information-packed, leisure and activity guides. Hundreds of suggestions for things to do and sights to see.

Alsace	1 84202 167 2
The Ardèche	1 84202 161 3
The Basque Country	1 84202 159 1
Brittany	1 84202 007 2
Catalonia	1 84202 099 4
Corsica	1 84202 100 1
The Dordogne & Périgord	1 84202 098 6
French Alps	1 84202 166 4
Languedoc-Roussillon	1 84202 008 0
Normandy	1 84202 097 8
Poitou-Charentes	1 84202 009 9
Provence & the Côte d'Azur	1 84202 006 4
Pyrenees & Gascony	1 84202 015 3
South West France	1 84202 014 5